Hamsha Raspberry Pi

Learn How To Use Raspberry Pi For Amateur Radio Activities And 3 DIY Projects

Introduction

I want to thank you and congratulate you for downloading the book, "*Hamshack Raspberry Pi: Learn How To Use Raspberry Pi For Amateur Radio Activities And 3 DIY Projects*".

This book has actionable information on Hamshack Raspberry Pi that will help you to learn how to use Raspberry Pi for amateur radio activities and much, much more.

Since you are reading this book, I'm sure you are enthusiastic about radio activities, if not about the revolutionary Raspberry Pi. I'm also sure there's so much you've heard about radio stations like tracking satellites, communicating in Morse code or perhaps playing a game over the air as well- and you want to try them out.

That's very possible, and you don't have to spend a lot of money to learn all that- and become a professional radio operator- because a cheap raspberry Pi computer and a couple of other cheap tools are all you require to begin your amateur radio journey.

Maybe you haven't been adequately introduced to the small computer known as Raspberry Pi; that is not a reason to skip reading this book because you will know everything –from the basics- about Pi, before we get to the actual playing with the Hamshack Raspberry Pi. Among other things, you will learn how to install, configure and use the device to enjoy some of the coolest things in tech today. For about $40, you will be able to enhance your knowledge of how to operate radio as an amateur; you will learn how to install different operating aids like time keeping, logging, Morse code practicing and satellite tracking. You will also learn about designing antennas, essential Ham programs like twclock and GNU radio companion, radio configuration tools and even how to set up your own ground station with simple steps!

Best of all, you'll be able to complete the projects discussed in the book by yourself without any problems because they are so damn easy and straightforward. Shall we begin?

Thanks again for downloading this book. I hope you enjoy it!

© **Copyright 2017 - All rights reserved.**

The contents of this book may not be reproduced, duplicated or transmitted without direct written permission from the author, Dwight Stanfield.

Under no circumstances will any legal responsibility or blame be held against the publisher for any reparation, damages, or monetary loss due to the information herein, either directly or indirectly.

Legal Notice:

This book is copyright protected. This is only for personal use. You cannot amend, distribute, sell, use, quote or paraphrase any part or the content within this book without the consent of the author.

Disclaimer Notice:

Please note the information contained within this document is for educational and entertainment purposes only. Every attempt has been made to provide accurate, up to date and reliable complete information. No warranties of any kind are expressed or implied. Readers acknowledge that the author is not engaging in the rendering of legal, financial, medical or professional advice. The content of this book has been derived from various sources. Please consult a licensed professional before attempting any techniques outlined in this book.

By reading this document, the reader agrees that under no circumstances are is the author responsible for any losses, direct or indirect, which are incurred as a result of the use of information contained within this document, including, but not limited to, —errors, omissions, or inaccuracies.

Table of Contents

Introduction

A Comprehensive Background of the Raspberry Pi

    What Is It?

    A Short History of Raspberry Pi, And the Setup

    Setting Up Your Raspberry Pi

    The Wi-Fi Set Up

    For this guide, we will connect to a Wi-Fi network with the information below:

Initial Software Installation

    Installing Samba

    Setting up the Printer

The Ham Radio Programs

    Gpredict – For Satellite Tracking

More Ham Radio Programs, And Projects

    GNU Radio Companion

Build a FlightAware PiAware Ground Station

Remote Ham Radio Operation Via Raspberry Pi

Conclusion

Let's start from the beginning i.e. understanding the Raspberry Pi before we get to the point of discussing various other issues surrounding the Raspberry Pi.

A Comprehensive Background of the Raspberry Pi

What Is It?

In simplest terms, the Raspberry Pi refers to a series of small computers (in the category of single board computers) that were developed in the UK by the Raspberry Foundation to help teach basic computer science in various schools both in the developed and developing countries. Out of the box, the new device, which you can purchase from Raspberrypi.org, comes without the peripheral devices (mouse, case and keyboard).

Before we discuss the specifics of how to set up and use the Raspberry Pi as a pro even as a complete beginner, we will start by going through the journey through time i.e. how the Raspberry Pi came into being. This short history will help you to understand Raspberry Pi well before we get to set it up.

A Short History of Raspberry Pi, And the Setup

Before raspberry Pi was invented, personal computers had become an expensive household appliance. Many parents had grown reluctant of letting their kids use the family computers due to the high cost of the machines and fragility. Many kids, as a result, were not well-versed with computers. In 2006, Dr. Eben Upton together with his associates from the University of Cambridge realized that there was a steep decline in numbers and skills of the students enrolling for computer science courses. They decided to develop an inexpensive computer that would enable young people familiarize themselves adequately with computer concepts.

In 2011, the Raspberry Pi Model B was created and it sold more than two million units within a period of two years. Since then, there has been an ongoing improvement in different models of Raspberry Pi.

The machine is not only a computer but a microcontroller as well with pins that can sense externally and actually control devices. The computer, among other uses, is used for general purpose computing, learning about programming, product prototyping, controlling robots, creating a media center, security systems and home automation, and as a project platform.

Setting Up Your Raspberry Pi

Obviously, before you set it up, you need to purchase your Raspberry Pi. Once you have your own Raspberry Pi, now you can go on to set it up. Luckily, setting up your Pi is pretty straightforward.

First of all, you have to make sure the Raspberry Pi operating system is installed on the SD card. You can do this using the NOOBS (new out of box software) program easily. The operating system of Raspberry Pi, known as Raspbian, and data storage are stored on a Micro SD card. This means that you can be able to set up different SD cards -each one of them booting a Raspberry Pi in different configurations. For instance, by changing the SD Card in the Pi, the device could be a robot, drone control system, camera controller, home security system, earthquake detector, weather station, radon detector, SETI cruncher, GPS, RFIDReader and many more.

You need to note that the micro SD card speed usually range up to class 10 (this is the fastest).

The class is indicated by a number in a circle. The recommended minimum useful class for Raspberry Pi is class 4. While the class 10 card will operate for a longer period of time, it (the card) tends to 'wear out' in time. Also, as with any computer data, you have to back up the SD card.

If you received your raspberry Pi pre-installed with a NOOBS SD card, you can very well skip to the Wi-Fi set up section in the book. Otherwise, you have to follow the steps below to download and install NOOBS on your SD card:

Go to this site and click the NOOBS icon. Select [Download Zip] and then unzip the folder containing the downloaded NOOBS system.

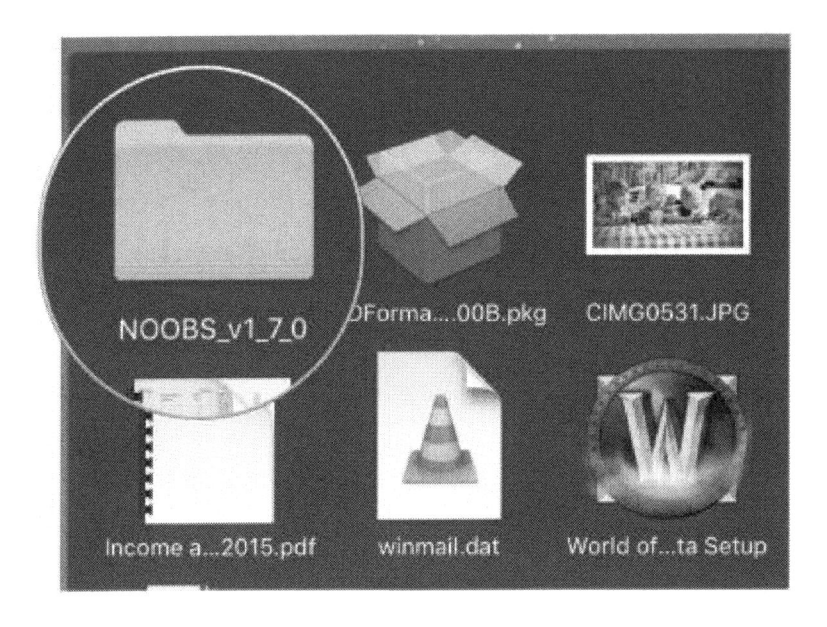

Follow the file labeled 'INSTRUCTIONS-README.txt' located in the unzipped NOOBS folder.

At the bottom of the desktop, you'll find the language selection window where you will choose the language of your country- for instance, in the US, select English. This will then lead to the display of the corresponding US keyboard. Now click on the Raspbian check box; click on the install icon, making sure to click 'yes' on the confirmation window. When the window labeled [OS(es) Installed] appears, just click OK.

The Wi-Fi Set Up

We will need to connect your device to the internet in order to download the programs in this book. The first step is to connect your device to a monitor and a keyboard. When you do so, login to the Raspberry Pi using these default Raspberry Pi credentials:

Username: pi
Password: raspberry

Get the network information

For this guide, we will connect to a Wi-Fi network with the information below:

- SSID (Network Name): Test Wifi Network
- PSK (Password): SecrectPassWord

Each time you see this password and network name in the guide, you have to change them to the password and network name for your local network. If you have to find the name of your local network, simply run the command below in your raspberry terminal:

sudo iwlist wlan0 scan

By doing so, you will get a list of all networks around you, and some important information for each network. You can however look for something that looks like ESSID: Test Wifi Network to find your network name.

Configure your network

You have to edit a file labeled *wpa_supplicant.conf.* to inform Pi to connect to your Wi-Fi network automatically. To open the file in nano, just type the command below:

Sudo nano /etc/wpa_supplicant/wpa_supplicant.conf

Scroll up to the end of the file, and then include the codes below to the file so that you are able to configure the network:

```
network={
  ssid="Test Wifi Network"
  psk="SecretPassWord"
}
```

Do not forget to replace it with your personal network name and password.

Press Ctrl+X followed by Y to save and close the file. Your device should now be able to connect to your network automatically. You can run the following command to check your network connection:

ifconfig wlan0

You will know you are connected when the output looks something like this:

```
wlan0  Link encap:Ethernet HWaddr 74:da:38:2b:1c:3d
       inet addr:192.168.1.216 Bcast:192.168.1.255 Mask:255.255.255.0
       inet6 addr: fe80::8727:5526:a190:b339/64 Scope:Link
       UP BROADCAST RUNNING MULTICAST MTU:1500 Metric:1
       RX packets:6917 errors:0 dropped:229 overruns:0 frame:0
       TX packets:2931 errors:0 dropped:1 overruns:0 carrier:0
       collisions:0 txqueuelen:1000
       RX bytes:10001000 (9.5 MiB) TX bytes:295067 (288.1 KiB)
```

In some instances, the device will not automatically connect; this means that you have to reboot to be able to do so. If it fails to connect after waiting 2-3 minutes, you could try rebooting the device using the command below:

sudo reboot

Download Your Free Bonus – [10 Best Ham Radio Websites](#)

Initial Software Installation

Installing Samba

Samba is a program that is important to install because you will need to share files with other computers on your local network. Using Pi as a samba file server is easy and with it, you'll also be able store backups from other computers.

Samba is basically the Linux implementation of CIFS (common internet file system) /SMB (server message block) file sharing standard used by windows computers and apple computers, and supported by games consoles, media streamers and mobile applications.

In this tutorial, I am assuming you have connected a keyboard, monitor and mouse to your Pi to set up your file server. I also assume you are using an SD card that offers a reasonable storage space without needing any additional steps to make it accessible. Nonetheless, if you require more storage, you can easily mount a large external USB drive and make a Samba entry for it.

Even though we've already set up the Wi-Fi, I would still recommend you use a wired Ethernet connection for fast transfer speeds and stability –especially if you are copying over large files (but the project will still work if you use the Wi-Fi).

Setting up Samba

Samba is basically available in the standard software repositories of Raspbian. We are now going to update the repository index, ensure the operating system is fully updated and install Samba with apt-get. Open the terminal and type the following:

sudo apt-get update

sudo apt-get upgrade

sudo apt-get install samba samba-common-bin

Create your directory

We are now going to make a dedicated shared directory on the micro SD hard disk. Even though you can put it anywhere, we'll put ours at the upper level of the root file system.

sudo mkdir -m 1777 /share

The command sets the sticky part to assist in preventing the directory from getting deleted accidentally and offers everyone the permissions to write/read/execute on it.

Configure Samba to share your directory

Configure Samba to share your new directory

```
# printer drivers
[print$]
   comment = Printer Drivers
   path = /var/lib/samba/printers
   browseable = yes
   read only = yes
   guest ok = no
# Uncomment to allow remote administration of Windows print drivers.
# You may need to replace 'lpadmin' with the name of the group your
# admin users are members of.
# Please note that you also need to set appropriate Unix permissions
# to the drivers directory for these users to have write rights in it
;   write list = root, @lpadmin

[share]
comment = Pi shared folder
path = /share
browseable = yes
writeable = yes
only guest = no
create mask = 0777
directory mask = 0777
public = yes
guest ok = yes
```

Now edit the config files of Samba to make the file share visible to the PCs on the network.

sudo leafpad /etc/samba/smb.conf

In this tutorial's example, you'll have to add the entry below:

```
[share]
Comment = Pi shared folder
Path = /share
Browseable = yes
Writeable = Yes
only guest = no
create mask = 0777
directory mask = 0777
Public = yes
Guest ok = yes
```

This simply means that anyone will be able to read, write and execute files in the share by either logging in as a Samba user (we'll set up that one below) or as a guest. If you don't want to allow guest users, you can omit the line 'guest ok=yes'.

You can also use Samba to share a the home directory of a user so that they are able to access it from somewhere else on the network, or share a bigger external hard disk which lives at a fixed mount point. Simply create an entry 'smb.conf' for any path that you want to share, and it will be availed across your network upon restarting Samba.

Creating a user and starting Samba

Before you start the server, you will have to set the Samba password, which is different from your standard default raspberry password. There's however no harm in wanting to use the same, because this is just a low-security, local network project.

```
sudo smbpasswd -a pi
```

As prompted, now set a password. Lastly, try to restart Samba:

```
sudo /etc/init.d/samba restart
```

From this point henceforth, Samba will automatically start each time you power on your Pi. Disconnect the monitor, mouse and keyboard safely after making sure that you can locate the shared network folder. Let the Pi run as a headless file server.

You will also be able to locate the Raspberry Pi file server (which is by default named RASPBERRYPI) from any device on your local network. If you left the `smb.conf`'s default settings as they are, it will show in a Windows network group known as WORKGROUP.

The next obligation we have before downloading the Ham programs is setting up the printer. Let's do that now.

Setting up the Printer

As you will realize, you will need a physical output when you are implementing the Ham radio projects and thus, having a printer on standby is a prerequisite.

Installing CUPS on your Pi and permitting remote access

To link a printer with Pi, we first have to install CUPS (Common Unix Printing System). At this point, you'll fire up your Pi then navigate to the terminal either via SSH or on the Pi itself.

You need to enter the command below at the terminal, to start installing CUPS:

```
sudo apt-get install cups
```

When the 'continue' prompt pops up, simply type Y and then tap enter. Please feel free to grab a cup of coffee because CUPS is quite a beefy install. When the base installation completes, you need to make some administrative changes. The first thing you have to do is add yourself to the user group that can access the printers or printer queue. The user group created by CUPS is known as 'lpadmin'. The Raspbian's default user (and the user that we are logged into) is 'pi'- you can however adjust the following command if you desire a different user to access the printer.

Type the following command at the terminal:

sudo usermod -a -G lpadmin pi

In case you are wondering, the switch labeled '-a' enables you to add an existing user (that is 'pi') to an existing group (that is 'lpadmin') as specified by the switch labeled '-G.'

The last part of the pre-configuration process is to enable the remote editing of CUPS configuration. You can complete the rest of the configuration through the web browser on your Raspberry Pi. If you want to, you are free to use your windows desktop browser to finish the configuration; all you will need is to toggle a bit of value in /etc/cups/cupsd.conf. Enter the command below at the terminal:

sudo nano /etc/cups/cupsd.conf

Now look for this section within the file:

Only listen for connections from the local machine
Listen localhost:631

Now comment out the line labeled 'Listen localhost:631' and replace it with the line below:

```
# Only listen for connections from the local machine
# Listen localhost:631
Port 631
```

This will instruct CUPS to start listening for all networking interface contacts, which are directed to the port 631. Make sure to scroll down further in the config file to get to the section that is labeled 'locations'. In the following block, I have bolded any lines that need to be added to the config:

```
< Location / >
# Restrict access to the server...
Order allow,deny
Allow @local
< /Location >

< Location /admin >
# Restrict access to the admin pages...
Order allow,deny
Allow @local
< /Location >

< Location /admin/conf >
AuthType Default
Require user @SYSTEM

# Restrict access to the configuration files...
Order allow,deny
Allow @local
< /Location >
```

The 'allow @local' line addition enables the access to CUPS from any computer on your local network. Each time you do any changes in the CUPS configuration file, you will have to restart the CUPS server. Use the command below to do that:

```
sudo /etc/init.d/cups restart
```

Once you restart CUPS, you should be able to access the administration panel through any of your local network's computer by pointing its web browser at this link: http://[the Pi's IP or hostname]:631.

Add a printer to CUPS

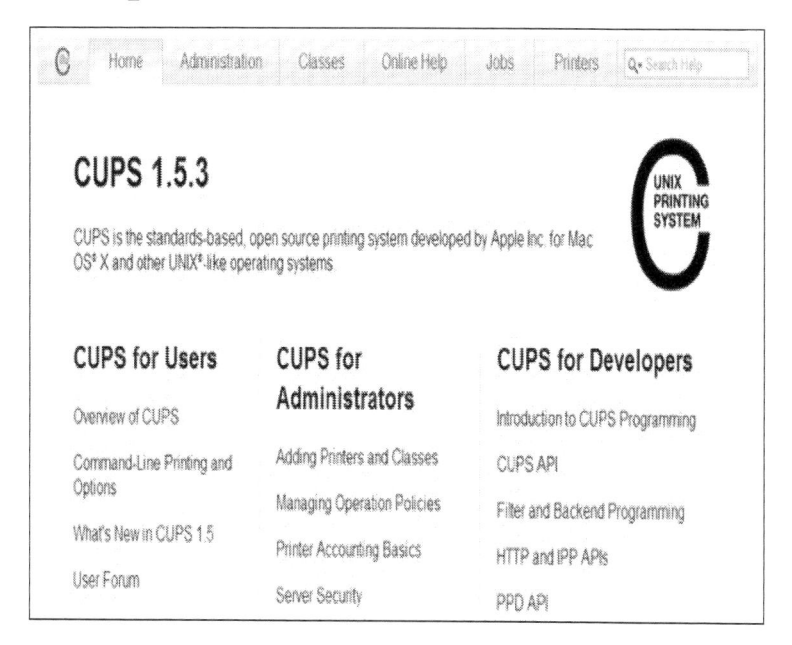

CUPS 1.5.3

CUPS is the standards-based, open source printing system developed by Apple Inc. for Mac OS® X and other UNIX®-like operating systems

CUPS for Users
- Overview of CUPS
- Command-Line Printing and Options
- What's New in CUPS 1.5
- User Forum

CUPS for Administrators
- Adding Printers and Classes
- Managing Operation Policies
- Printer Accounting Basics
- Server Security

CUPS for Developers
- Introduction to CUPS Programming
- CUPS API
- Filter and Backend Programming
- HTTP and IPP APIs
- PPD API

When you navigate to this link: http://[the Pi's IP or hostname]:631 ,you will be able to see the CUPS homepage, as illustrated in the image above. However, are interested in the 'administration' tab so click on it.

Next, click 'add printer' in the administration panel. If you get a warning regarding the security certificate of the site, you can ignore it by clicking 'proceed anyway'. You'll be prompted to enter a username as well as the password.

> **Authentication Required**
>
> The server https://192.168.1.100:631 requires a username and password. The server says: CUPS.
>
> User Name: pi
> Password: ********
>
> [Log In] [Cancel]

Proceed and enter the username details as well as the password of the account that you added to the 'lpadmin' group earlier on in the tutorial. For instance, if you chose to use the raspbian install (the default), the login as well as the password should be 'Pi' and 'raspberry' respectively. Now click on log in. Once you log in, you will see all the printers available (those that are local and the networked at the same time). Choose the printer you want to add to the system.

Add Printer

Local Printers:	○ HP Printer (HPLIP)
	○ HP Fax (HPLIP)
Discovered Network Printers:	◉ Brother HL-2170W series (Brother HL-2170W serie
Other Network Printers:	○ AppSocket/HP JetDirect
	○ Internet Printing Protocol (ipp)
	○ Backend Error Handler
	○ LPD/LPR Host or Printer
	○ Internet Printing Protocol (https)
	○ Internet Printing Protocol (ipps)
	○ Internet Printing Protocol (http)
	○ Windows Printer via SAMBA

[Continue]

Once you choose the printer, you'll be given the chance to edit the description, location and name of the printer, and also to enable network sharing. Since the printer we're using is already a network printer, we didn't check the 'share this printer' box.

Add Printer

Name: Brother_HL-2170W_series
(May contain any printable characters except "/", "#", and space)

Description: Brother HL-2170W series
(Human-readable description such as "HP LaserJet with Duplexer")

Location: Office
(Human-readable location such as "Lab 1")

Connection: dnssd://Brother%20HL-2170W%20series._pdl-datastream._tcp.local/

Sharing: ☐ Share This Printer

[Continue]

Once you edit the name of the printer and add a location, you will get a prompt to choose the specific driver that you want for your printer. While it discovered the printer and printer name automatically, CUPS doesn't make any attempt to choose the correct driver for you. After installing the right driver, scroll down until you are able to see a model number matching your own. As an alternative, if you have a PPD file for the printer that you've downloaded from the manufacturer, simply load it with the button labeled 'choose file'

Add Printer

Name: Brother_HL-2170W_series
Description: Brother HL-2170W series
Location: Office
Connection: dnssd://Brother%20HL-2170W%20series._pdl-datastream._tc
Sharing: Do Not Share This Printer
Make: Brother [Select Another Make/Manufacturer]
Model:
- Brother HL-2170W Foomatic/hl1250 (en)
- **Brother HL-2170W Foomatic/hpijs-pcl5e (recommended) (en)**
- Brother HL-2170W Foomatic/hpijs-pcl5e (recommended) (en)
- Brother HL-2170W Foomatic/lj4dith (en)
- Brother HL-2170W Foomatic/lj4dith (en)
- Brother HL-2170W Foomatic/ljet4 (en)
- Brother HL-2170W Foomatic/ljet4 (en)
- Brother HL-2170W Foomatic/ljet4d (en)
- Brother HL-2170W Foomatic/ljet4d (en)
- Brother HL-2400CeN Foomatic/hl1250 (recommended) (en)

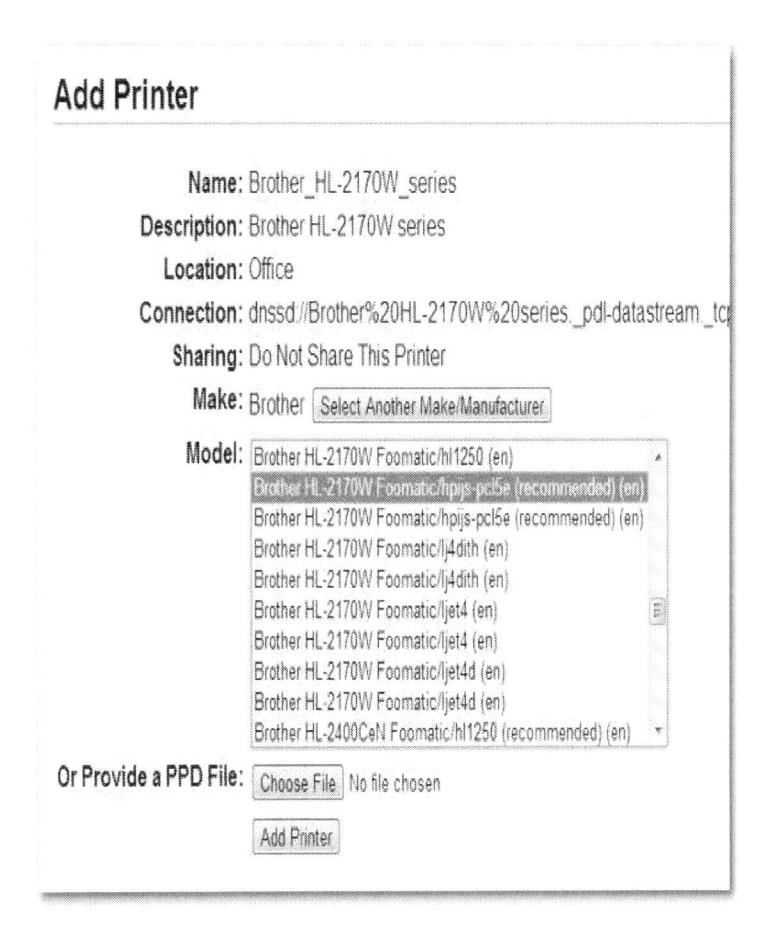

Or Provide a PPD File: [Choose File] No file chosen

[Add Printer]

The final step entails looking over general print settings such as the name and address of your preferred/default printer. the default paper source or size and so forth. It ought to default to the right presets, even though it never hurts to check though.

Once you click the 'set default options', you'll be able to see the printer's default administration page (this is for the printer you added to the CUPS system).

All looks well. The real test, nonetheless, is actually getting to print something. Fire up the default text editor of Raspbian, Leafpad, and send a message:

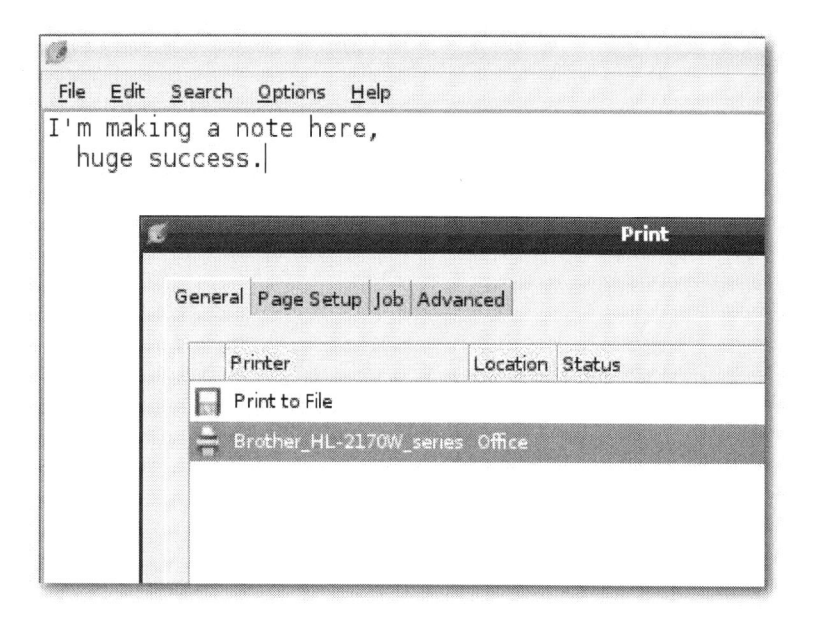

So far, if you have included the only user that has to access the printer to the 'lpadmin' group, and you have also added or included the only printer you want to access the CUPS system, that should be it. If you've got other users or additional printers you would want to add, just run through the individual steps that we've just discussed above to do so.

The Ham Radio Programs

We will now discuss the installation of important Linux amateur radio software. You can find the list of these software at http://www.raspberryconnect.com/raspbian-packages-list/item/71-raspbian-hamradio.

Hamradiomenus (it Establishes Menus)

Let's first take an overview of this program:

This program creates a sub-menu for the applications of Ham radio that you have installed. The program only appears when you have installed at least one application with a desktop entry file that contains the category entry: *HamRadio*.

The program does not have any additional hardware requirements.

How to install it

There are two ways of installing the software that you can choose from:

Start by opening a terminal session; on the taskbar, click on the terminal icon at the upper part of the screen.

There are two ways to install software. Choose one of the following methods:

Using the command line to install it

If you've not recently done an update, you can do so for new and updated Linux packages currently available with:

$ sudo apt-get update

If a new package version installed on your machine is available, the package will be upgraded with the command below. We don't have any installed packages that are ever removed by the command.

$ sudo apt-get upgrade

Tap the enter key when you get a prompt asking you if you want to continue.

Now type the command below to install the program:

$ sudo apt-get install hamradiomenus

Likewise, when you get a prompt asking you if you want to continue, tap the enter key. Once the download is complete, you have completed the installation.

Using the add or remove software menu selection

On the task bar, find the Raspberry icon and click on it. On the drop down menu that appears, click on preferences. Choose add or remove software and then enter HamRadioMenus in the search box and tap enter. Click the *hamradio menus for KDE and GNOME* selection square and click on the Apply button. Input the Pi password and when the download is complete, it means the installation is complete as well.

NOTE:

- The Hamradiomenus does not require a desktop entry.

- Configuration is also not needed.

- With regards to its operating, when a HamRadio category application is installed, the HamRadio menus icon appears

Aldo- Morse Code

Aldo is a learning tool in Morse code that provides four kinds of training methods shown as the startup menu. And they include the following:

- Blocks method- this one is used to identify different blocks that have random characters that are played in Morse code

- Koch- this is where two characters are played at top speed until you can pinpoint 90% of them, then another character is included and so forth.

- Read from file – entails sending characters that are produced from a file.

- Call sign- entails identifying random call signs played in Morse code

- Settings- setting up speed and techniques of selecting letters to be sent

- Exit program

The program does not have extra hardware requirements. For the installation however, you have two methods to choose from:

Installation by the command line

Open a terminal session by clicking the icon on the terminal on the task bar at the top of the screen. If you've not recently updated the information about the new, updated Linux packages that are available, please do so using:

$ sudo apt-get update

If a new version of a package that is installed on your machine is available, it will be upgraded with the command below. You should note that there aren't any installed packages that are ever taken away by the command.

$ sudo apt-get upgrade

In order to install the program, use:

$ sudo apt-get install aldo

When you get a prompt asking you whether you want to continue, tap the enter key. The installation will be complete when the downloading is done.

The installation by add or remove software menu selection

First click on the icon on the taskbar symbolizing Raspberry. On the drop down menu that appears, click on preferences. Now choose add or remove software and in the search box, enter aldo and tap enter. There will be a selection square labeled Morse Code training program; click on it. Click on the apply button and enter the Pi password. The installation will be complete when the download is done.

NOTE:

For the desktop entry- type the following to be able to generate a start menu window for aldo:$ sudo nano /usr/share/applications/aldo.desktop in the resulting editor:

Download Your Free Bonus – 10 Best Ham Radio Websites

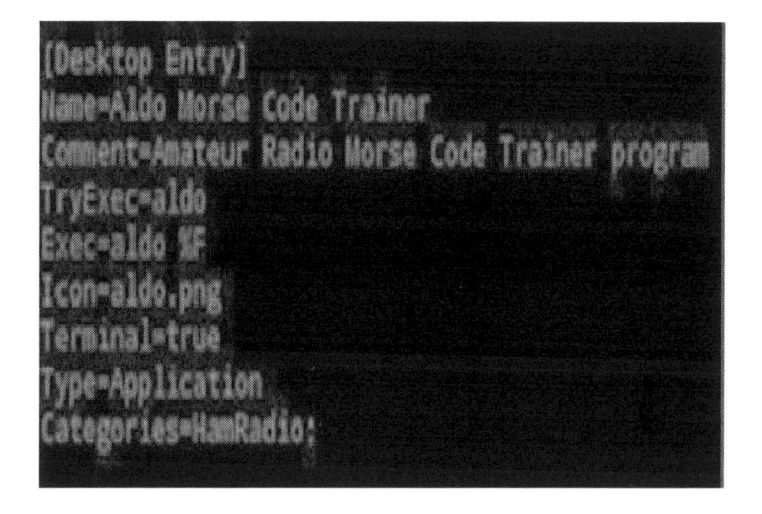

```
[Desktop Entry]
Name=Aldo Morse Code Trainer
Comment=Amateur Radio Morse Code Trainer program
TryExec=aldo
Exec=aldo %F
Icon=aldo.png
Terminal=true
Type=Application
Categories=HamRadio;
```

Type "[Ctrl] X","Y" then enter to save the file then restart the menu by typing:

$ sudo lxpanelctl restart

For the configuration, select option 5, which refers to the setup, and then select option one for the Keyer Setup. Press the enter key twice after which the different parameters can be set. Once you complete the program setup, option 6 will take you to the main menu.

For the operating, simply click menu-HamRadio-Morse Code Training and then choose the code type you want to have generated. If you are using a HDMI HD TV as the monitor, you will hear the sound from the speaker of the monitor, or the monitor's audio output jack if the monitor doesn't have a speaker.

Chirp- configuration tool for amateur radios

Chirp is basically a tool meant for restoring, saving and management of memory, and preset data in the amateur radios. It basically supports many manufacturers and models, and also offers a way to interface with various data sources and formats. You can find the supported radio models in the site below.

http://chirp.danplanet.com/projects/chirp/wiki/Supported_Radios

For the hardware, this program will require a USB cable to connect with your device. Please see here for more information.

For the installation, you have two ways at your disposal to do that (choose one):

Installation by the command line

Open a terminal session by tapping on the terminal icon at the top of the screen (on the task bar). If you've not updated the information about the new and updated Linux packages that are available, use:

$ sudo apt-get update

If a new version of a package installed on your machine is available, the command below will be used to upgrade the package. As usual, there are no packages that have ever been erased by this command.

$ sudo apt-get upgrade

Now in order to install the program, use:

$ sudo apt-get install chirp

You will receive a prompt asking you whether you want to continue- press enter. You will know the installation is complete when the download is complete.

Installation by add or remove software menu selection

On your taskbar, simply click on the raspberry icon; on the drop down menu that appears, choose add or remove software, and in the search box, enter chirp; now press enter. You will see a selection square labeled 'configuration tool for amateur radios' click on the apply button then enter the Pi password.

You will know the installation is complete when the downloading is done.

Desktop entry file: this one is generated automatically.

Configuration: the program does not require any initial configuration.

With regards to the operation, you can use this guide.

When the download is complete, you have completed the installation.

Fldigi- the Digital Modem Program

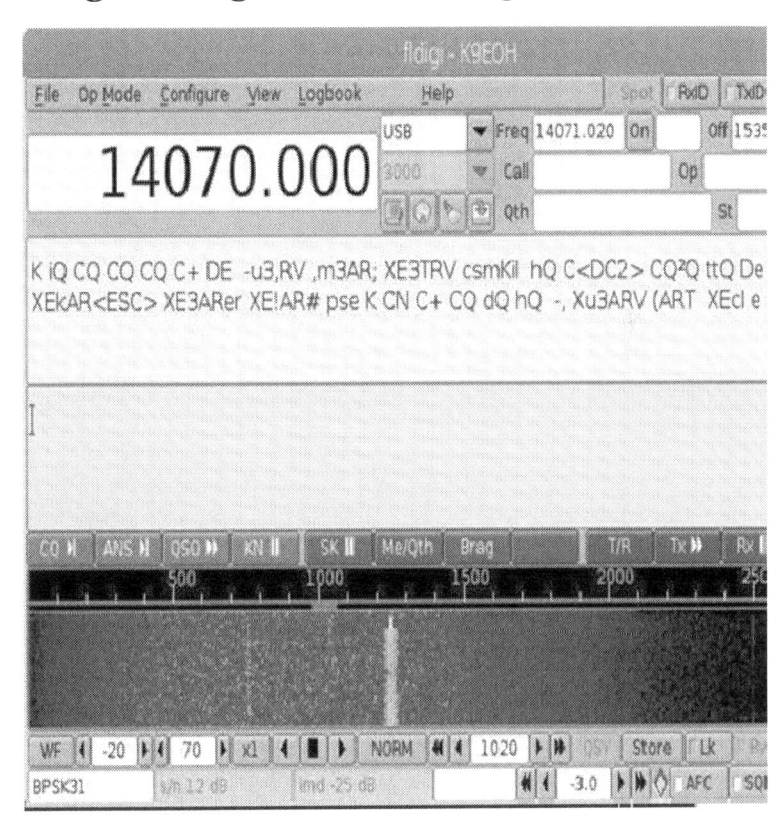

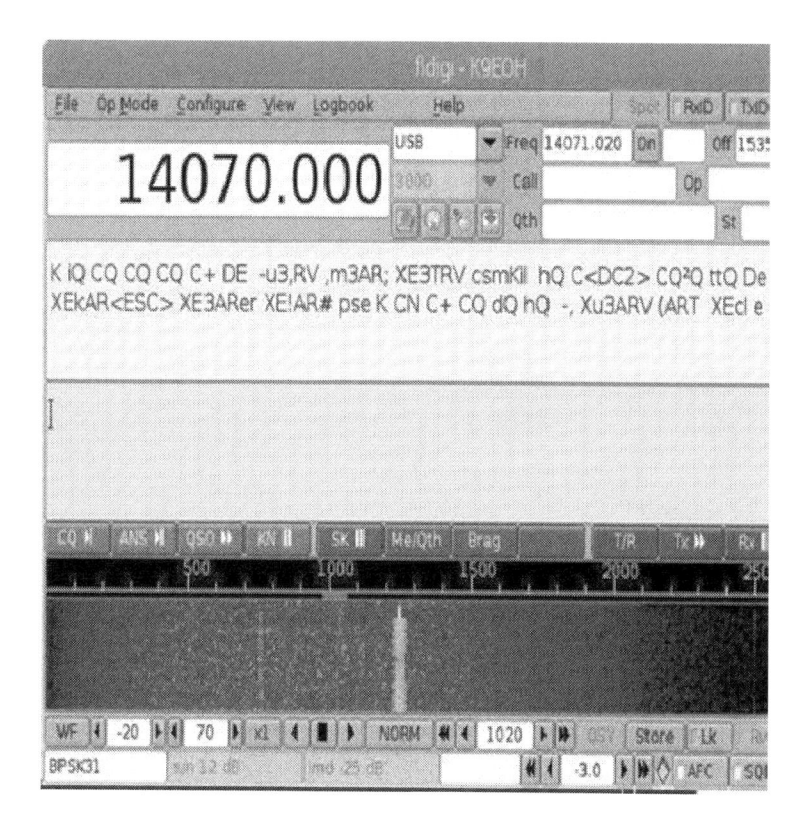

The image above describes the Fldigi screen.

Fldigi is basically a modem program that supports most current digital modes that are used by ham radio radio operators. You can also use the program to do a frequency measurement test or calibrate your sound card to WWV. This program also has a CW decoder. When you start open flarq you get a correction of errors in transmission caused by the subsequent ability to transmit as wekk as receive Automatic Repeat Request (ARQ) frames. But what is Flarq?

Flarq (fast light automatic repeat request) is an ARQ specification based file transfer application that has the capacity to transmit and receive ARQ data frames through MultiaPsk on windows or Fldigi on Linux.

Flmsg on the other hand is a management editor, which is best suited for amateur radio supported standard formats of message that include MARS, ICS, HICS, NTSRadiograms, Red Cross, plain text and IARU. Its data files are ASCII that can be transmitted from one point to another via amateur radio, the internet or other electronic links.

Flwrap is a little desktop app encapsulating an image file, text file or a binary file inside a group of identifier blocks. This app is created for use to its fullest with fldigi even though you can also use it with any digital model program.

Let's now look at the hardware.

As you may have noticed, raspberry pi doesn't have an audio input capability and so you'll require an external audio adapter like the Tigertronics Signal Link USB. If you have a computer assisted transceiver (CAT), it means that the fldigi software and the transceiver will be able to pass the info to and fro. In the instance the transceiver frequency is altered, the fldigi display will also indicate and you can use it to enter the time and frequency information automatically in the built-in logging program in fldigi. A cable is needed for the CAT function (and probably the manufacturer has a cable available for you to connect the transceiver to the computer) so you should check with your transceiver's distributor to get this cable.

Nonetheless, these cables normally use RS-232 specifications. You would probably also require a RS-232 TO USB adapter for the Pi connection. Just go to Amazon.com or a similar site and enter *RS-232 TO USB adapter* and search.

NOTE/CAUTION:

The program creates a complete duty cycle with high levels of modulation when used on the air using transmitting equipment.

You thus have to refer to the manual of your transceiver and reduce the output power of your transmitter to a safe level.

For the installation, there are two ways to choose from:

Installation using the command line

Just click on the terminal icon located on the taskbar on top of your screen to open a terminal session. If you have not updated the info about new and updated packages of linux, you can do so using:

`$ sudo apt-get update`

(To get the available packages at the moment)

In the case that a new package version installed on your machine is available, the command below will be used to upgrade the package. There are no installed packages that are ever erased by this command though.

Installation by adding or removing the software menu selection

On the task bar, click on the Raspberry icon; on the drop down list that appears, click on preferences then choose add or remove software.

You will see a search box; enter fldigi then press enter, then click the selection squares labeled:

'digital modem program for hamradio operators',

'amateur radio file encapsulation/compression utility' and

'ham radio transceiver control program.'

Next, tap on the button labeled 'apply'; you might also be requested to enter the pi password. When the download finishes, it means the installation has finished as well.

As regards to the desktop entry file, you have to note that Fldigi and Flarq are both bundled in this package. The desktop entry files for both of them are created automatically. Nonetheless, network is included along with the Ham Radio category. In case you desire to remove the network entry, use:

```
$ sudo nano /usr/share/applications/fldigi.desktop
```

In the editor, remove network that results; from the line of categories with these results:

```
[Desktop Entry]
Name=Fldigi
GenericName=Amateur Radio Digital Modem
Comment=Amateur Radio Sound Card Communications
Exec=fldigi
Icon=fldigi
Terminal=false
Type=Application
Categories=HamRadio;
```

To save the file, press "[Ctrl] X", "Y" and press enter. repeat this for the desktop entries:

$ sudo nano /usr/share/applications/flmsg.desktop$ sudo nano /usr/share/applications/flwrap.desktop$ sudo nano /usr/share/applications/flarq.desktopUpdate the Menus:$ sudo lxpanelctl restart

As regards to the configuration, you have to note that connecting the audio interface and the transceiver control cable is important (if you are using them) before you open fldigi. The first time the program is run, you will see some 'Fldigi configuration wizard' displayed. Now tap on next.

Download Your Free Bonus – [10 Best Ham Radio Websites](#)

Now enter your call sign, Location, Name, locator or maidenhead locator

Enter your Callsign, Name, Location (QTH), Maidenhead locator and antenna info. Tap on next.

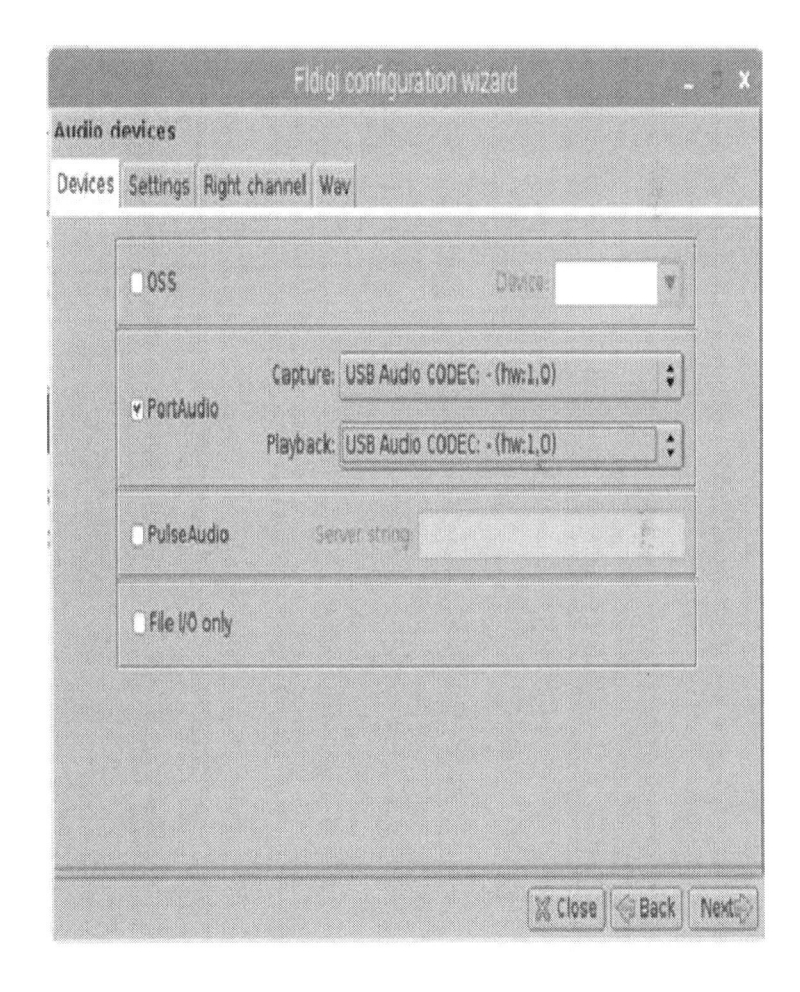

Click on the tab labeled 'devices' for SignaLink USB interface and then check the Port

AudioBox; choose USB Audio CODEC: USB Audio (hw:1,0) for capture; choose USB Audio CODEC: USB Audio (hw:1,0) for Playback and select right channel tab.

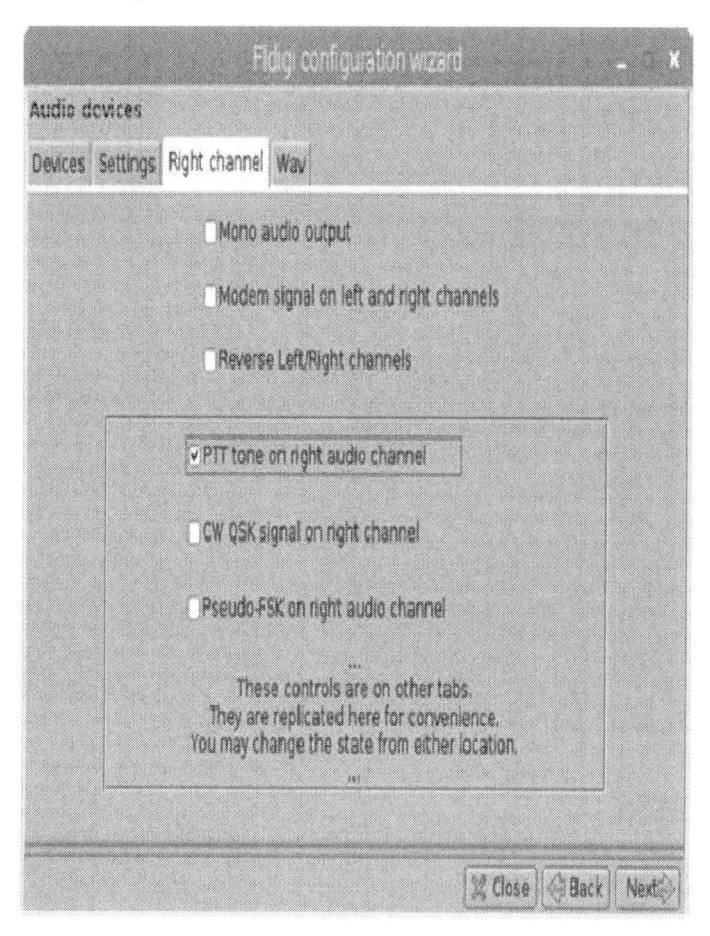

Now click the *right channel* tab and choose 'PTT tone on the right audio channel' before clicking on next. Click on the Hamlib tab in the transceiver control window.

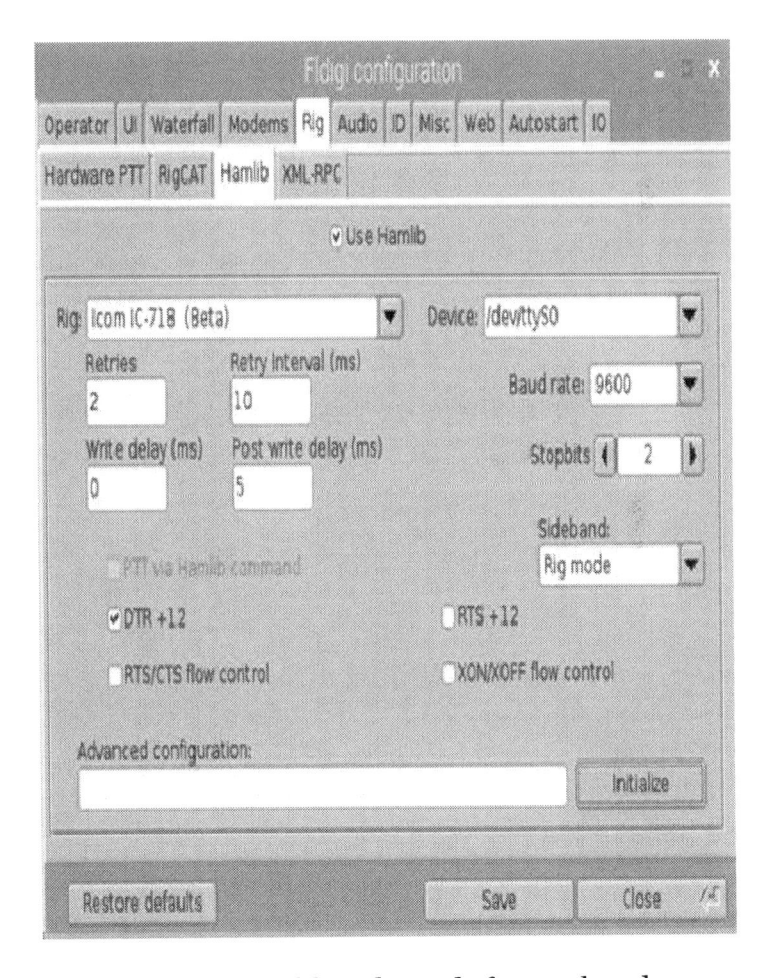

Choose the Hamlib tab and from the drop down menu that appears, choose your rig. Choose /dev/ttyS0 (under device- drop down menu). Next, set the Baud rate for your rig. You may need to experiment with the four boxes labeled RTS+12, DTR+12, the XON/XOFF flow control as well as the RTS/CTSflow control so that you push the Hamlib to operate your rig. Now click on the checkbox labeled 'Hamlib' and then click the 'initialize' button as well. Tap on next until the program starts. At the top of the fldigi window, you'll find 'configure selection'; click on it too.

On the drop down window, click on Misc and then on CPU; confirm that the slow CPU box is left unchecked if you know you are using a Raspberry Pi that is either 700 MHz or faster than that. After that click on the 'NBEMS' tab- if you wish for the incoming messages to be displayed on a flmsg form, ensure you check the 'open with flmsg' checkbox. If you would want a copy to be put in a browser HTML format as well, click on the checkbox labeled 'open in browser'.

Now move to the taskbar and click on the terminal icon to open a terminal session. You can enter the command below to find the location of flmsg:

```
$ sudo find / -name flmsg
```

```
pi@HAMSHACK:~ $ sudo find / -name flmsg
/usr/share/doc/flmsg
/usr/bin/flmsg
```

As you can see from the image above, go ahead and key in the line- /usr/bin/flmsg- which does not contain /doc/ in the flmsg: window. Click one save and close then click on the 'x' in the upper right corner to restart the program. You will need to click on the button labeled 'yes' as well to confirm quit.

After that, choose fldigi through the menu system in the task bar at the top of your screen (raspberry icon), Fldigi and HamRadio.

As regards to the operating, the digital brands include the following:

1.805-1.838, 3.522-3.620, 7.025-7080, 10,137-10.142,14.070-14.107, 18.098-18.106, 21.070-21.540, 24.197-24.922 and 28.076-28.120 MHz.

You can get the full list along with the modes here:

Gpredict – For Satellite Tracking

Gpredict is an application for real-time orbit prediction and satellite tracking. This application can track numerous number of satellites and show their position and related data in tables, lists, maps and if course polar plots.

The app can also be able to make predictions of a satellite's time for future passes and offers you all the information about all passes.

Gpredict has been seen as being a unique satellite tracking program because it enables you to assemble the satellites in terms of visualizations modules, and you can configure each one of them (the modules) independently from the others, thus offering you unlimited flexibility with regards to the look and feel of the modules. Naturally, Gpredict also allows you to track satellites comparatively to various observer locations all at the same time.

The installation and usage

Start the terminal window and type the following command:

```
sudo apt-get install gpredict
```

Your Raspberry device will then download and install the software for you and take you back to the command prompt when it completes.

To start up the software, just type the following from your terminal window:

```
gpredict
```

With that, the software now starts up; you have to perform a bit of configuration to let the program to know your current location (Copenhagen- is the default).

Click edit or preferences and choose the ground stations tab. Then press add new and proceed to add your location details, altitude, longitude and latitude. Once you save that, you can now delete the sample location of Copenhagen and turn your own into the default.

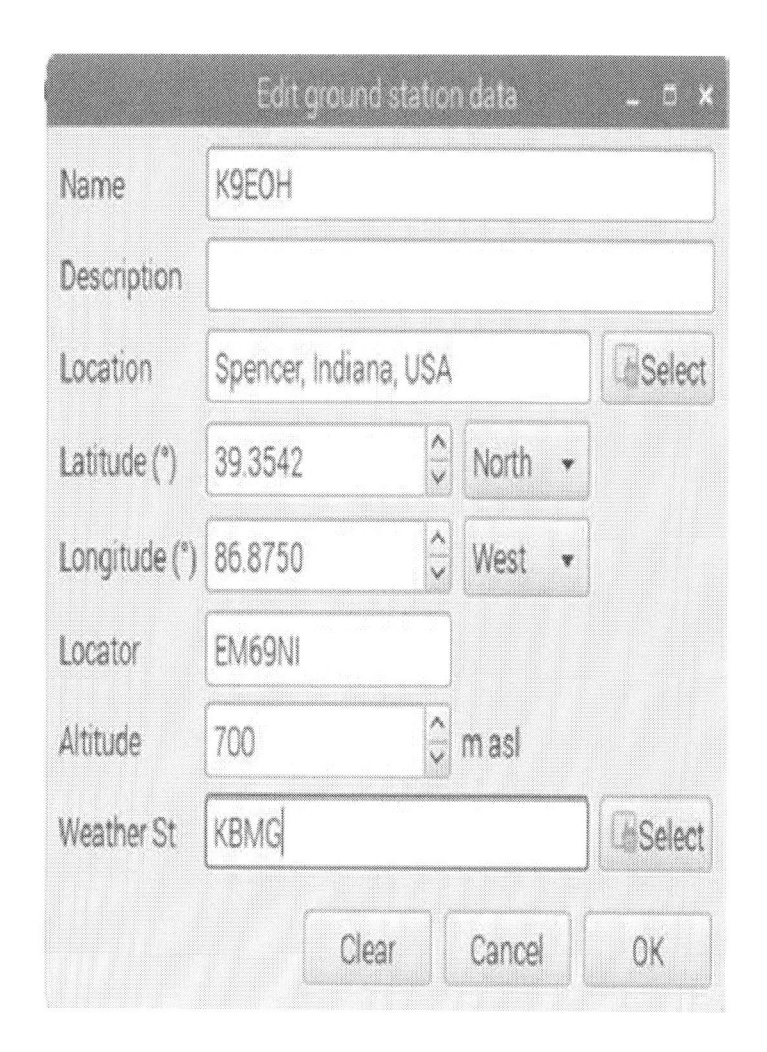

While still in preferences, you can choose your screen layout. If you have a large monitor, then the optimum is table, Map, Polar and a wide single sat (you however have the freedom to play around and see the one that suits you best). You may have to restart the program for the changes to take effect.

About now, it might be a good idea to check that you've got the latest satellite data, which the program can download for you. Select Edit/Update TLE from network and then give it a moment for the update to finish.

Lastly, you will want to configure the satellites that you are tracking. The software will default to the amateur radio module. Just click on the options or shortcuts on the module –at the top right area of the main window, right beneath the main windows control: close, maximize and minimize. Just click on that and then configure.

Once you do all that, you can now select the satellites you want to track. While Fancube-1 or even AO-73 is not being displayed under those names, you can search for it and include it- it is believed to be 2013-066B though. I personally included other satellites like ISS, VO-52, FO-29 and SO-50. Your choice may be different.

At this point, you should be able to see the location of all your satellites as plotted on the screen.

If you want more details about a specific satellite, simply highlight it in the list at the bottom and right click to choose 'future passes' or 'show next pass.'

I can say that G-predict does work well on the Pi. Even though it doesn't appear to max the processor out really well, at least it is quick to start up and shut down- if you want to engage yourself with something else.

Twclock- world clock

As a ham operator, the clock program will prove to be very helpful. Apart from displaying GMT and local time, it is able to display the current time of all the major cities around the globe. It also has an alarm to inform you when the time for a station ID arrives.

As you will realize, you can set the ID alarm to a preferred delay of seconds and minutes. The alarm will inform you that it's time to ID or all of the ways below:

- Beep the PC's speaker
- Blink the alarm button
- Send a call in CW to you using pulseaudio via your sound card

You could feed the CW audio to your rig to allow transmission of the ID is automatically. The CW is produced using code from qrq.

You will also find an auto reset choice. This choice starts the next time out automatically without any action from you, the user.

So, you need to connect your soundcard's output to the 'audio-in' pin of your rig's accessory jack so that it is transmitted.

Essentially, this program is essentially a clock that is tailored for the ham radio operators, those who want to know the time in some other place in the world, or just about anyone who has had enough of the same look of the ordinary clock. The program shows the current date and time in different cities around the world at the same time.

The installation

The installation process is simple, and it uses the CLI (command line interface).

Begin by updating the repository index on your Raspberry Pi by using:

```
Sudo apt-get update
```

Now search for the Raspberry Pi repository index for the twclock programs via:

```
Apt-cache search twclock
```

Next, install the program:

```
Sudo apt-get install twclock
```

When that is done, start twclock. In the graphic user interface of your computer, open the top left application menu and choose accessories, twclock. You can open two programs of twclock at the same time- one of them set to local time and the other one to GMT time.

Uninstalling it is also simple:

```
sudo apt-get uninstall twclock
```

So far, you have pretty much enough programs to get you started with amateur radio activities. However, since you have to be really good at this, I will add a couple more, under the next chapter in which we will look at full Ham projects.

Download Your Free Bonus – [10 Best Ham Radio Websites](#)

More Ham Radio Programs, And Projects

GNU Radio Companion

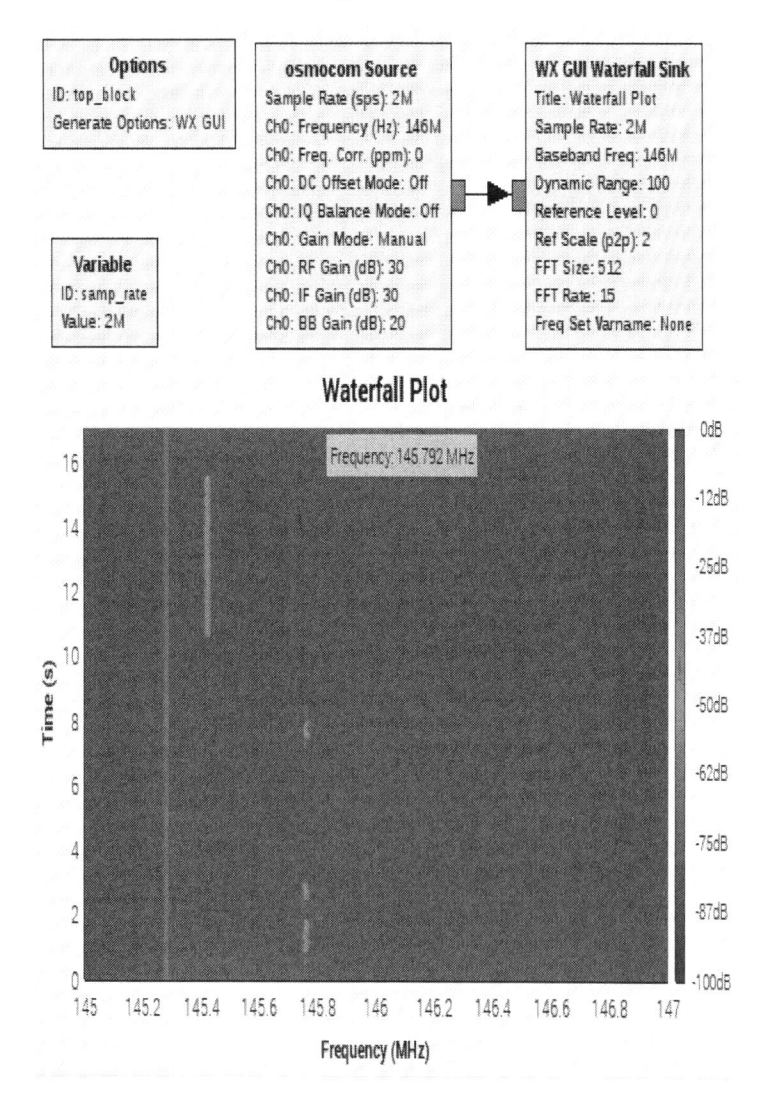

Options
ID: top_block
Generate Options: WX GUI

Variable
ID: samp_rate
Value: 2M

osmocom Source
Sample Rate (sps): 2M
Ch0: Frequency (Hz): 146M
Ch0: Freq. Corr. (ppm): 0
Ch0: DC Offset Mode: Off
Ch0: IQ Balance Mode: Off
Ch0: Gain Mode: Manual
Ch0: RF Gain (dB): 30
Ch0: IF Gain (dB): 30
Ch0: BB Gain (dB): 20

WX GUI Waterfall Sink
Title: Waterfall Plot
Sample Rate: 2M
Baseband Freq: 146M
Dynamic Range: 100
Reference Level: 0
Ref Scale (p2p): 2
FFT Size: 512
FFT Rate: 15
Freq Set Varname: None

Waterfall Plot

Frequency: 145.792 MHz

GNU Radio is basically a free software development toolkit that essentially offers blocks to implement software radios. You can use it with readily available cheap external RF hardware to build software defined radios or in an environment resembling a simulation without any hardware. This software is mainly used by commercial and academic environments, and hobbyists as well to support real-world radio systems and wireless communications research.

The applications of GNU radio are mainly written with Python programming language, and the supplied performance-critical path of signal processing is usually implemented in C++ with, where available, processor floating point extensions. This means that the developer is capable of implementing radio systems, which are real time and high throughput in a rapid-application development environment that is simple to use.

Even though GNU is not primarily a simulation tool, it supports development of signal processing algorithms with pre-recorded or generated data- which avoids the necessity of having actual RF hardware. The package also contains a graphical tool known as gnuradio-companion, which creates signal flow graphs and generates flow-graph source code as well. We also have many different tools and a utility program included.

Why do you need GNU?

GNU Radio does all the signal processing; you can write applications with it to get data out or even push data into the digital streams, which is then transmitted via hardware. A GNU radio contains channel codes, filters, synchronization elements, vocoders, demodulators, equalizers and other elements (we usually refer to these as blocks in the GNU jargon) that are usually located in radio systems. More importantly, it also has a way of connecting blocks and can manage the way data usually passes from one block to another. It is actually very easy to extend a GNU Radio: if you get a particular missing block, you can create it and add it quickly.

Moving on;

GRC (GNU Radio companion) is a graphical user interface that is used in the development of GNU Radio applications. As you can see in the images above, you can use some inexpensive SDR USB dongles (>$20) such as the NooElec R820T SDR & DVB-T NESDR Mini (more on this later).

You can use the process below to install it using the command line interface:

Update the raspberry Pi repository index using:

Sudo apt-get update

Now make a search in the Raspberry Pi repository index for Gpredict programs with:

Apt-cache search gnuradio

- pi@raspberrypi:~ $ apt-cache search gnuradio
- gnuradio - GNU Radio Software Radio Toolkit
- gnuradio-dev - GNU Software Defined Radio toolkit development
- gnuradio-doc - GNU Software Defined Radio toolkit documentation
- gr-air-modes - Gnuradio Mode-S/ADS-B radio
- gr-fcdproplus - Funcube Dongle Pro Plus controller for GNU Radio
- gr-osmosdr - Gnuradio blocks from the OsmoSDR project
- libair-modes0 - Gnuradio Mode-S/ADS-B radio
- libgnuradio-analog3.7.5 - gnuradio analog functions
- libgnuradio-atsc3.7.5 - gnuradio atsc functions
- libgnuradio-audio3.7.5 - gnuradio audio functions
- libgnuradio-blocks3.7.5 - gnuradio blocks functions
- libgnuradio-channels3.7.5 - gnuradio channels functions
- libgnuradio-comedi3.7.5 - gnuradio comedi instrument control functions
- libgnuradio-digital3.7.5 - gnuradio digital communications functions
- libgnuradio-dtv3.7.5 - gnuradio digital TV signal processing blocks
- libgnuradio-fcd3.7.5 - gnuradio FunCube Dongle support
- libgnuradio-fcdproplus0 - Funcube Dongle Pro Plus controller for GNU Radio
- libgnuradio-fec3.7.5 - gnuradio forward error correction support
- libgnuradio-fft3.7.5 - gnuradio fast Fourier transform functions
- libgnuradio-filter3.7.5 - gnuradio filter functions
- libgnuradio-iqbalance0 - GNU Radio Blind IQ imbalance estimator and correction

Install gnuradio with:

Sudo apt-get install gnuradio

Next, install gr-osmosdr with:

Sudo apt-get install gr-osmosdr

Install gr-air-modes with:

Sudo apt-get install gr-air-modes

Now start GRC- In your desktop's GUI, select programing, GRC (after opening the top left application). Make a GRC 2 meter (146 MHz) waterfall plot with a SDR.

Plug in the device below to the Pi: (you can find more details about it from NooElec).

I personally used a USB hub for the device because it is too large and would thus block the rest of the USB ports.

Now drag the RTL-SDR Source (in sources) to the left work window. Drag the WX GUI Waterfall sink (in instruments, WX) to the left work window.

Now wire the source output of osmacom to WX GUI Waterfall Sink.

In the variable and ID same_rate, alter the value to 2 MS/s

In the source output of osmacom to the WX GUI Waterfall sink, alter the frequency to the values: 146E6.

In the top icon menu, choose 'generate the flow graph.'

Save the file in the file menu.

Finally, choose execute the flow graph in the top icon menu.

The set up

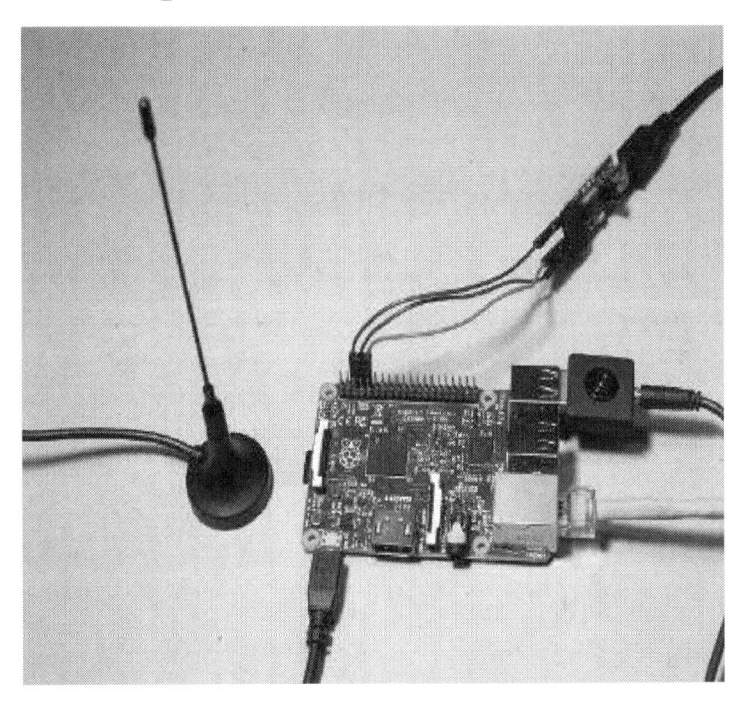

It always seems quite amazing to me what a humble USB TV dongle can do- considering you can pick up one for about £10 together with the open source SDR software. As you can see in the picture above, it is very simple to plug one of them in one of the USB ports, with the supplied antenna fixed. Please visit this page for more information about RTL-SDR.

Now that we are re-purposing a TV tuner which the Linux kernel supports, and which it would otherwise claim and for television reception, we have to first of all make the kernel to stop doing so. We will edit the '**/etc/modprobe.d/raspi-blacklist.conf**' file and proceed to add the following line below:

blacklist dvb_usb_rtl28xxu

Install Software (RTL-SDR)and the GNU Radio support as follows:

$ sudo apt-get install rtl-sdr gr-osmosdr

You will also require setting up a new udev rule so that you are able to access the device as a non-root user- you however first have to ascertain the USB ID. Make sure the tuner is plugged in and then type the following:

$ lsusb

This should give you the following:

Bus 001 Device 004: ID 0bda:2832 Realtek Semiconductor Corp. RTL2832U DVB-T

Now you need to create the /etc/udev/rules.d/20.rtlsdr.rules file with the following line:

```
SUBSYSTEM=="usb",                ATTRS{idVendor}=="obda",
ATTRS{idProduct}=="2832",   GROUP="adm",   MODE="0666",
SYMLINK+="rtl_sdr"
```

At this point, you can restart Udev; nonetheless, since you also had a kernel module blacklisted, you probably should consider rebooting as the easiest way.

The test

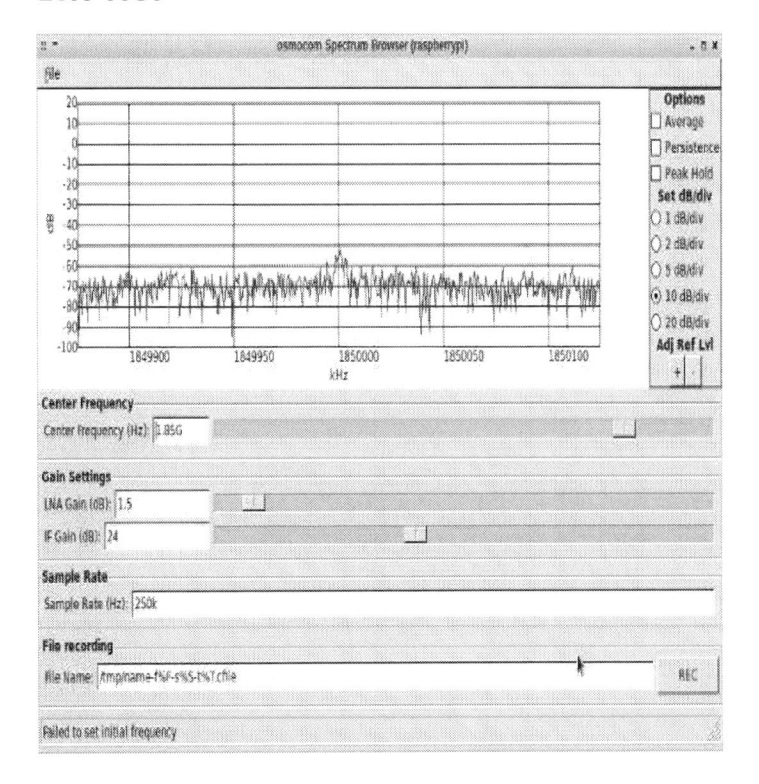

You can run the FTT application to get a modest spectrum display, which is offered as part of the gr-osmocom software.

```
$ osmocom_fft
```

If you then look at the CPU load, you can see that you've got a lot of capacity to spare, with just a single core at about 70% utilization.

```
top - 14:21:22 up 14 min,  3 users,  load average: 1.86, 0.69, 0.40
Tasks:  83 total,   2 running,  81 sleeping,   0 stopped,   0 zombie
%Cpu(s): 17.2 us,  1.3 sy,  0.0 ni, 81.3 id,  0.0 wa,  0.0 hi,  0.2 si,  0.0 st
KiB Mem:    764060 total,   203720 used,   560340 free,    17100 buffers
KiB Swap:   102396 total,        0 used,   102396 free,   102792 cached

  PID USER      PR  NI  VIRT  RES  SHR S %CPU %MEM    TIME+ COMMAND
 2189 pi        20   0  286m  99m  53m R 70.4 13.4   3:54.14 osmocom_fft
 2103 pi        20   0 10176 3488 2856 S  3.3  0.5   0:22.10 sshd
 2185 pi        20   0  4948 2464 2100 R  0.7  0.3   0:03.64 top
   43 root      20   0     0    0    0 S  0.3  0.0   0:00.54 kworker/0:1
    1 root      20   0  2248 1332 1232 S  0.0  0.2   0:01.69 init
```

The gr-air-modes

Over the recent past, so much has been written about how to use the RTL-SDR hardware along with the GNU Radio-based gr-air-modes software, to get position and the heading information from the aircraft Mode-S transponders. While many writers state that they tried using a Raspberry Pi Model B (and a laptop)- this hasn't proven to have enough processing power and the result is usually buffer underruns.

A couple more dependencies are needed, in order to build gr-air-modes.

```
$ sudo apt-get install cmake libboost-dev sqlite pyqt4-dev-tools liblog4cpp5-dev swig
```

Having installed these ones, the sources can be cloned from GitHub as follows:

$ git clone Github

To then create and install:

```
$ cd gr-air-modes
$ mkdir build
$ cd build
$ cmake ../
$ make
$ sudo make install
$ sudo ldconfig
```

You can now use the following to run the application:

$ modes_rx -s osmocom

And with only a small antenna and a significant number of miles from the closest airport, you will still manage to receive no shortage of output.

```
pi@raspberrypi ~ $
pi@raspberrypi ~ $ modes_rx -s osmocom
linux; GNU C++ version 4.9.1; Boost_105500; UHD_003.007.003-0-unknown

gr-osmosdr 0.1.3 (0.1.3) gnuradio 3.7.5
built-in source types: file osmosdr fcd rtl rtl_tcp uhd miri hackrf bladerf rfspace airspy
Using device #0 Realtek RTL2832U SN: 00000991
Found Elonics E4000 tuner
Invalid sample rate: 4000000 Hz
Gain is 34
Rate is 4000000
Using Volk machine: generic_orc
(-40 0.00000000) No handler for message type 24 from 5b44c1
(-36 0.00000000) Type 4 (short surveillance altitude reply) from 5125f at 87700ft (GROUND ALERT)
(-36 0.00000000) Type 0 (short A-A surveillance) from 648693 at 200ft (speed <75kt)
(-37 0.00000000) Type 4 (short surveillance altitude reply) from 4ee766 at 38300ft (AIRBORNE ALERT)
(-39 0.00000000) Type 4 (short surveillance altitude reply) from 4d3bf at 125500ft (AIRBORNE ALERT)
(-41 0.00000000) No handler for message type 24 from 4f5d0c
(-36 0.00000000) Type 0 (short A-A surveillance) from 4d6e4a at 12400ft (No TCAS)
(-38 0.00000000) Type 5 (short surveillance ident reply) from 5lebf with ident 242 (AIRBORNE ALERT)
(-35 0.00000000) Type 5 (short surveillance ident reply) from a0bc2c with ident 134 (aircraft is on the ground)
(-35 0.00000000) Type 4 (short surveillance altitude reply) from 330fce at 3425ft (SPI ALERT)
(-38 0.00000000) Type 0 (short A-A surveillance) from a54ae6 at 31500ft (speed 75-150kt)
(-37 0.00000000) Type 5 (short surveillance ident reply) from 0fc7c1 with ident 1300 (AIRBORNE ALERT)
(-40 0.00000000) Type 4 (short surveillance altitude reply) from c966c8 at 1700ft (SPI)
(-40 0.00000000) Type 0 (short A-A surveillance) from 43c86d at 53400ft (No TCAS)
(-41 0.00000000) No handler for message type 24 from c02d66
(-40 0.00000000) Type 5 (short surveillance ident reply) from a79fe0 with ident 6108 (SPI)
(-35 0.00000000) Type 0 (short A-A surveillance) from ae43d7 at 96800ft (TCAS resolution inhibited)
```

Once again, not to mention, with a lot of headroom to spare:

```
top - 09:28:22 up 10:23,  3 users,  load average: 0.50, 0.37, 0.19
Tasks:  83 total,   1 running,  82 sleeping,   0 stopped,   0 zombie
%Cpu(s):  5.4 us,  1.2 sy,  0.0 ni, 92.4 id,  0.9 wa,  0.0 hi,  0.0 si,  0.0 st
KiB Mem:    764060 total,   318912 used,   445148 free,    27420 buffers
KiB Swap:   102396 total,        0 used,   102396 free,   207648 cached

  PID USER      PR  NI  VIRT  RES  SHR S %CPU %MEM    TIME+ COMMAND
 9067 pi        20   0  202m  80m  40m S 25.2 10.7  0:08.57 modes_rx
 9086 pi        20   0  4948 2524 2156 R  0.7  0.3  0:00.14 top
   57 root      20   0     0    0    0 S  0.3  0.0  0:00.25 kworker/2:1
    1 root      20   0  2556 1364 1256 S  0.0  0.2  0:02.40 init
    2 root      20   0     0    0    0 S  0.0  0.0  0:00.00 kthreadd
    3 root      20   0     0    0    0 S  0.0  0.0  0:00.09 ksoftirqd/0
    5 root       0 -20     0    0    0 S  0.0  0.0  0:00.00 kworker/0:0H
```

Build a FlightAware PiAware Ground Station

You can construct and actually run your ADS-B ground station which you can install anywhere and actually receive data in real time on your computer directly from airplanes. Your ground station will be able to run FlightAware's PiAware software to be able to track any flights that are within a 100-300 mile radius (this is the line of sight- the range depends on the antenna installation) and will feed data to FlightAware automatically. You can track flights off your PiAware gadget directly or through FlightAware.com.

NOTE: As a token of appreciation from FlightAware, you will receive the following for sending ADS-B data:

- Live data through flightaware.com- this is subject to a delay of standard data processing of up to two minutes.

- An access to live data (that is up-to-the-second) that is received by the local device (this is accessible with a local network connection from the stats page).

- Data from the local device highlighted on the track logs of FlightAware.

- Detailed site performance statistics.

- A free <u>enterprise account</u> for just $89.95 per month

Getting started

The process is quick and very easy. With the instructions below, you'll find the process short- it actually takes about 2 hours to complete the project- the parts themselves cost about $100.

Apart from your Pi, and other essentials we've already discussed like an SD card, you will need the following:

USB SDR ADS-B (Automatic Dependent Surveillance-Broadcast) Receiver (Pro Stick Plus or FlightAware recommended)

The USB SDR ADS-B receiver will transform the 1090 MHz radio signal to a form that your computer can actually understand

TIP: if you are selecting between the Pro Stick Plus and FlightAware Pro Stick, remember that the Plus contains an on-board filter which works very well in places that contain a lot of radio noise- like urban environments.

1090 MHz Antenna

To start, you can buy an indoor antenna. If you are using the FlightAware USB adapter, ensure the antenna contains an SMA connector.

If you are using a telescoping mast antenna, make sure to break it down to a quarter wave length of 1090 MHz -6.9 cm- so that you maximize reception.

Download Your Free Bonus – [10 Best Ham Radio Websites](#)

Install PiAware on your SD card

I will now show you how to install the software on your SD card if you are using a windows or Mac OS; however, I have to remind you to ensure you select the right drive to install the image.

1. Windows

Download the PiAware software on Raspbian Linux ZIP whose size is 310 MB then save the file on your computer. By clicking the link, it downloads the file into your computer's download folder automatically.

Next, visit https://etcher.io/ to download the SD card writer (which is about 80MB) in size and follow the directions to install the program.

You can find the info about your windows OS under Control Panel >all control panel items> system. To see all the control panel options, view the control panel with little icons.

▸ Control Panel ▸ All Control Panel Items ▸ System

Next, open Etcher. You may have to run Etcher as administrator. To do so, right click \run as administrator\

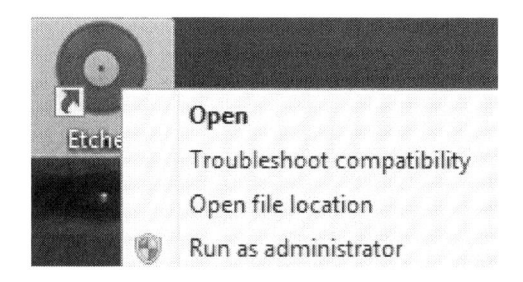

Choose the PiAware zip file

Choose the correct Micro SD card USB drive carefully. This process usually overwrites any data that's on the drive so be careful with it to ensure you don't lose data accidentally. For instance, you can consider ejecting the external hard drives as well as any other storage devices to eliminate any likelihood of overwriting the data by accident.

On 'my computer' screen, confirm the drive. In the picture below, the removable disk (F) is the micro SD card:

When you are sure that the correct drive is selected, click 'flash!'

Once the PiAware has been installed, Etcher should actually automatically eject your SD card automatically; otherwise, you should manually eject your SD card then remove it from your computer if this doesn't happen.

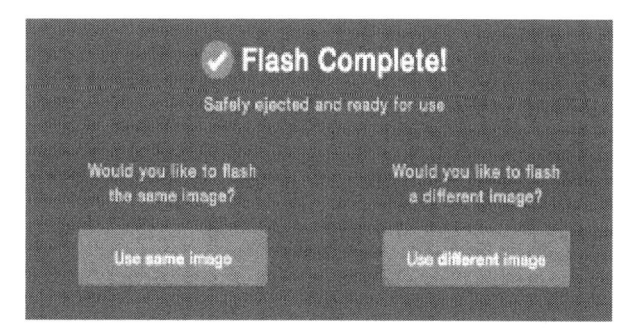

2. *Mac OS X*

Start by downloading PiAware on Raspbian ZIP, which is 310 MBs large. Save the file on your computer. Like I mentioned earlier, the file will download into your 'downloads' folder once you click on the link.

Next, visit https://etcher.io/ to download the SD card writer, which is about 80 MB in size and while following the directions indicated, install the program.

Now open etcher; you may have to run the program as administrator (use control + open application)

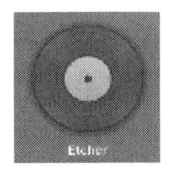

Now select the PiAware zip file and carefully choose the right Micro SD card USB drive carefully as you run the risk of overwriting important data. To avoid overwriting the data accidentally, simply remove any connected external hard drives.

On the 'finder' screen, confirm the drive. As you can see in the image below, the micro SD card is shown as 'NO NAME'.

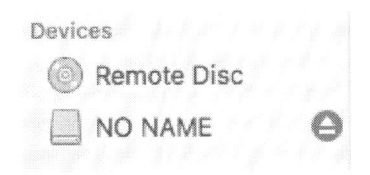

You will need administrative privileges on the computer- if a prompt appears, sign into an administrative account.

When you are sure the right drive is selected, press 'Flash!'

Once PiAware is installed, Etcher should eject the SD card automatically; otherwise, you can manually eject the card and remove it from your computer.

Start your PiAware device

Slide the SD card containing PiAware into your Pi.

You can also put the case on the Pi- this is optional though.

Plug the USB SDR ADS-B receiver into your Pi.

Plug the antenna cable into the USB SDR ADS-B dongle tightly.

If you are not using Wi-Fi, plug the internet cable (Ethernet) in (otherwise, you can skip this part).

Plug the power into your Pi.

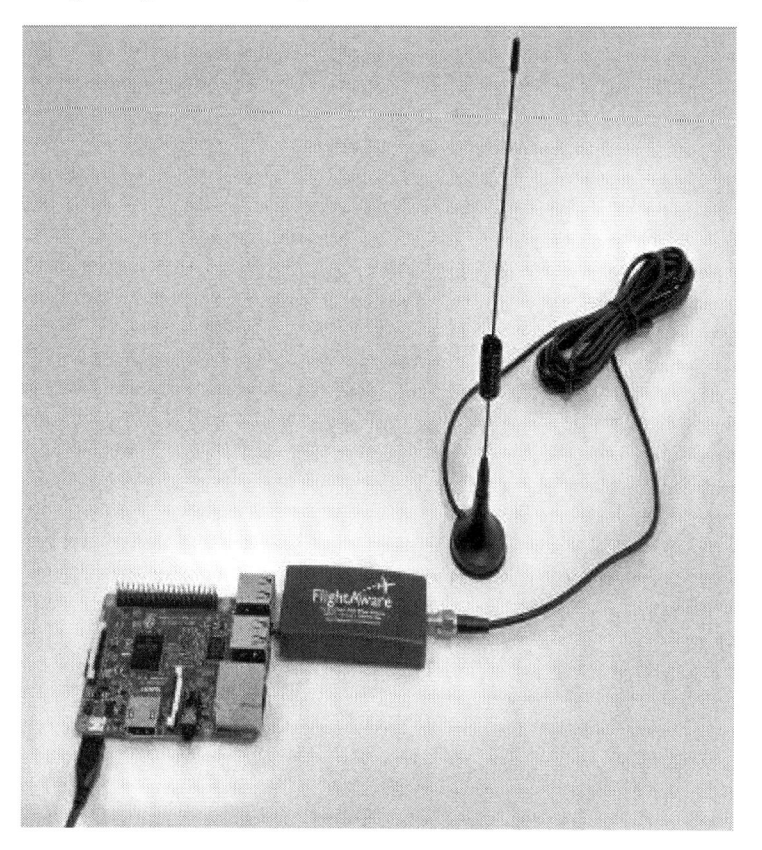

Make sure you see a solid red LED and also a blinking green LED on your Pi as well green and yellow LEDs next to the Ethernet jack.

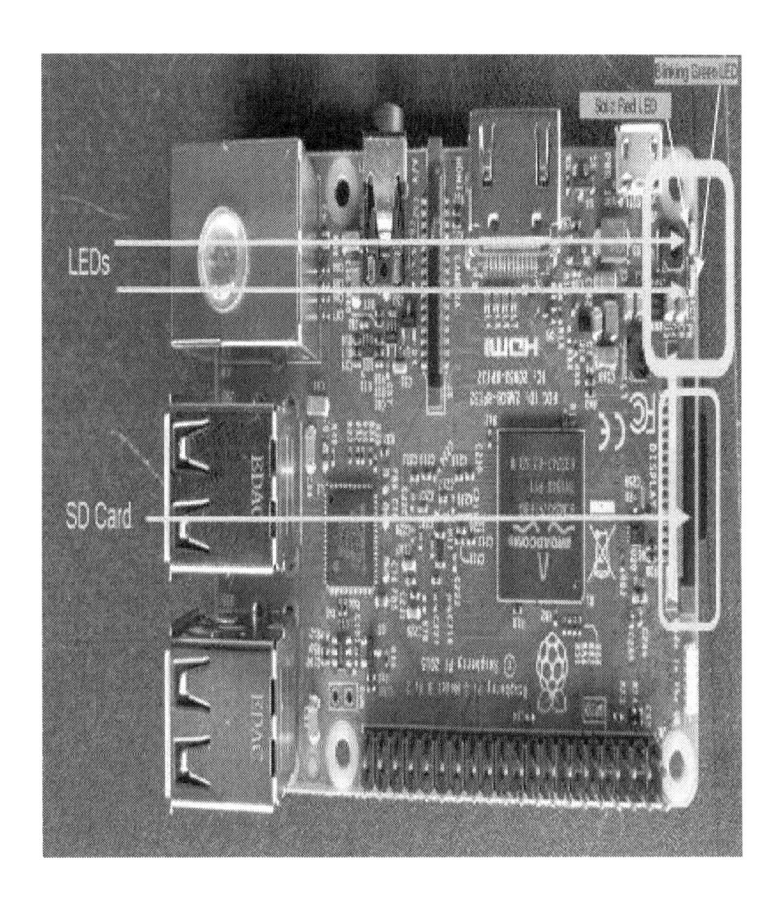

Get PiAware client on FlightAware.com

Give PiAware 4-5 minutes to start, and then you can link your FlightAware account with the PiAware device in order to get all the benefits.

When your device begins running, do the following:

Look up the IP address in your router admin and then go to the assigned IP address on the same network in a browser. If the device has not been claimed, you will get a display of the link to claim PiAware device.

Alternatively visit FlightAware.com to get your PiAware client.

If after five minutes your device has not been displayed as claimed, you can try to restart the device; if that does not work, you can reconfirm the accuracy of Wi-Fi settings (if you are using Wi-Fi).

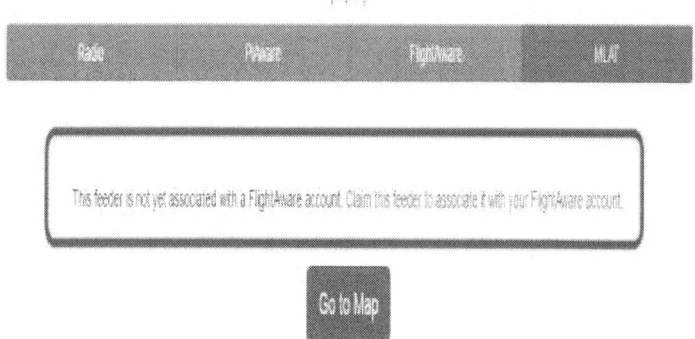

View your ADS-B statistics

Visit https://uk.flightaware.com/adsb/stats to see your ADS-B stats.

FlightAware will start to process your data as immediately and display your statistics in 30 minutes.

Click on the gear icon situated to the right of the Site name to configure your antenna height and location on your statistics page. Multilateration, which is also known as MLAT, works by pinpointing the aircraft location by knowing the site locations that got messages from the aircraft.

The stats page of FlightAware also tells you about your device's local IP and offers a link for direct connection. This is where you can get a link to SkyView- this is a web portal for observing flights that the receiver is getting messages from on a map.

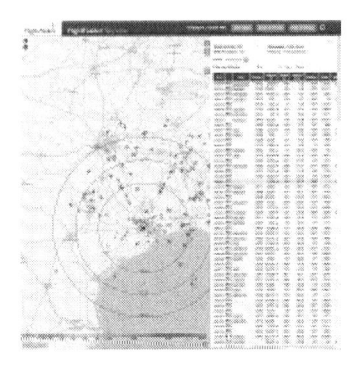

Congratulations!

Don't forget that the signals from the aircraft are not made to go through objects; this means that you should ensure the antenna is located in 'line of sight' to the sky without any obstructions. As you may realize, the most optimum installations, which are usually installed on a roof outdoors, contain a range of over 400km/250 mi.

Now that you are done, PiAware is yours to enjoy, and so is FlightAware, which comes with extra features that are exclusively reserved for feeders of ADS-B like you.

Remote Ham Radio Operation Via Raspberry Pi

In this project, you'll learn how to use your Raspberry Pi to set up a remote operation on your ham radio. In this case, you will use your Wi-Fi network, and VPN to make this possible.

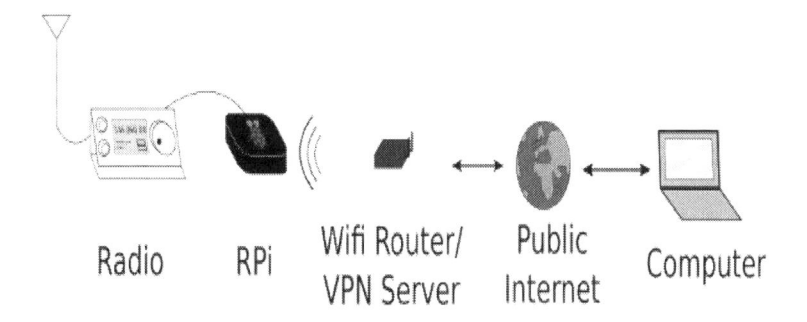

Why this is important

If you are a person who travels a lot and want to still continue using your rig even when you are away, this will prove important. Also, if you are a person who wants to set up your radio as well as the antenna away from where you live e.g. you are an apartment dweller and have parents or friends who stay in the boonies and would allow you to erect an antenna.

You will require the following to complete this project:

- ICOM-7100 all-mode radio
- Buffalo DD-WRT router/VPN server
- Raspberry Pi B+,
- Laptop that runs Ubuntu 15.04

NOTE: In this post, we'll focus on radio control and networked audio but not so much about setting up the VPN.

The basics

For this project, we want our raspberry to remain a 'headless' remote server. This means we don't need a keyboard or screen. You thus have to be able to SSH from your client into it. This is simple. You can set up private/public keys so that you don't have to type a password each time you log in. Just follow the link to set that up.

Build a PulseAudio 6.0 on your Pi

You have to use the PulseAudio Linux sound system in order to pipe the audio over the network. PulseAudio 2.0 occurs in the Raspberry Pi repositories. You first need to install some build dependencies:

sudo apt-get install -y libltdl-dev libsamplerate0-dev libsndfile1-dev libglib2.0-dev libasound2-dev libavahi-client-dev libspeexdsp-dev liborc-0.4-dev libbluetooth-dev intltool libtdb-dev libssl-dev libudev-dev libjson0-dev bluez-firmware bluez-utils libbluetooth-dev bluez-alsa libsbc-dev libcap-dev checkinstall

There is a libjson-c dependency you can build yourself:

git clone git://github.com/json-c/json-c.git

cd json-c

./autogen.sh

./configure

make

sudo make install

The clean pulse files that you may need to install:

(You need to note that this may break the other installed packages such as pygame).

```
sudo apt-get remove libpulse0
```

Next, acquire the PulseAudio source code; compile it. You can use checkinstall so that you can remove the built package easily later on.

```
git clone git://anongit.freedesktop.org/pulseaudio/pulseaudio

cd pulseaudio

./bootstrap.sh

./configure --prefix=/usr --sysconfdir=/etc --localstatedir=/var --disable-bluez4 --disable-rpath --with-module-dir=/usr/lib/pulse/modules

make

sudo checkinstall --pkgversion 6.0 --fstrans=no

sudo addgroup --system pulse

sudo adduser --system --ingroup pulse --home /var/run/pulse pulse

sudo addgroup --system pulse-access

sudo adduser pulse audio

sudo adduser root pulse-access
```

After that, you have to build the init.d script in order to get pulseaudio to start automatically in system mode- while this is not recommended, it makes a lot of sense on Pi. Proceed to Reboot to start PulseAudio or simply enter:

sudo service pulseaudio start

The configuration of PulseAudio to pass sound through the network

On Pi, simply edit the file /etc/pulse/system.pa, uncomment or include a line in order to turn on the module-native-protocol-tcp, to allow the local network to communicate with it.

Enable networked audio

load-module module-native-protocol-tcp auth-ip-acl=127.0.0.1;192.168.0.0/16

You may also find it great to comment out the module-suspend-on-idle line in it because it produced 10 seconds lags at first. Simply plug in the radio into your Pi and then proceed to restart PulseAudio with the following:

sudo service pulseaudio restart

Configure PulseAudio on the client

PulseAudio runs on a basis of 'per-user' on Ubuntu; not in system mode. In this case therefore, we can turn off and on the modules with scripts and that's what you'll do. Create a script and put in it commands like so:

```sh
#!/bin/sh


pactl load-module module-tunnel-source server=raspberrypi source_name=icom_source

pactl load-module module-tunnel-sink server=raspberrypi sink_name=icom_sink


# radio -> laptop speakers
pactl load-module module-loopback source=icom_source

# laptop microphone -> radio
pactl load-module module-loopback sink=icom_sink source=alsa_input.usb-0d8c_C-Media_USB_Audio_Device-00-Device.analog-mono
```

You need to adjust your Pi's hostname (or simply directly type its IP address in). You also have to adjust the second loopback module source. It is set to the USB microphone; but the microphone of your laptop will certainly be different. Now use the command below to obtain a list of sources on your computer and pick the name of the one you desire.

```
pacmd list-sources
```

Make your script executable by keying in the following:

```
chmod +x radio_pulse.sh
```

In this script, you can also enable networking, but you might also find it very convenient to apply the paperfs program and select the option below:

'Make the discoverable PulseAudio network sound devices available locally'.

Lastly, you've got to set up authentication. PulseAudio makes use of a shared secret that's referred to as cookie for authentication. Simply copy the cookie from the Pi at /run/pulse/.config/pulse/cookie to ~/.pulses-cookie in the home directory. It will now authenticate.

On your client, restart PulseAudio using:

```
pulseaudio -k && sudo alsa force-reload
```

Now run the above script; if everything goes on well, you will now hear the sound from your laptop's radio. You also have to make a couple of adjustments within the pavucontrol program. Make sure to turn the radio down squelch so that there is something that comes through. Next, click on the playback tab and then click show all streams and ensure the loopback from Pi is playing on gadget you want it to play on. This is what it should look like:

You can run pavucontrol for the Raspberry Pi as well from your client as follows:

PULSE_SERVER=raspberrypi pavucontrol

You can then adjust the Pi connections if you find it necessary.

You should ensure you set your device to DATA mode (or FM-D) if you are using an IC- 7100, or in a way that your USB audio gets into the transmitter. You can now do digital modes and voice through your network- how cool is that! Take a look at the image below that shows running fldigi on a laptop that is receiving audio in this setup:

Remember that at this point, you are on a local network and so you'll have to create the VPN to go outside your house via the internet.

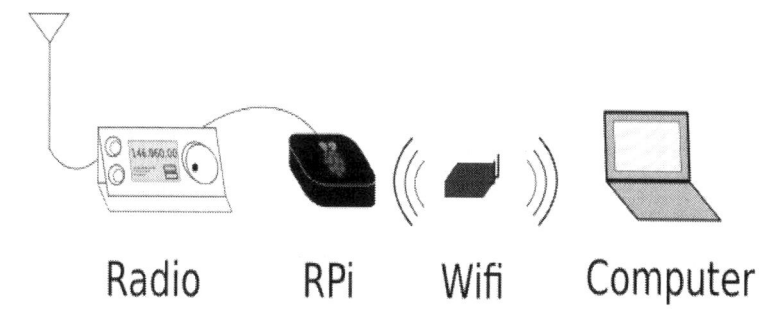

Radio   RPi   Wifi   Computer

Control the radio from far

If you only want to conduct digital modes through fldigi, you probably are good to go at this point. You can run flrig on Pi and fldigi on the client, and they'll be able to connect and key up the radio and things like that. But what if you want to do voice as well, what do you do?

If you are a programming nerd, you can write your own small controller for IC-7100 in a language like Python. You'll find it simple, and will allow you to switch the radio on and off, switch the DATA mode on and off, access the different memory channels and key up the radio. This is a good start but you can make it a lot more sophisticated with time. You will particularly need to be able to key in the frequency you want or scan down or up the bands for HF; something that should not be too difficult to add. You can feel free to use it if you want but do not expect a lot; if you want to improve it, go ahead!

We have other programs out there offering the ability to control a radio via the network.

Troubleshooting

I personally went through quite a number of iterations and found numerous problems as I tried to figure it all out. I conducted the PulseRadio configurations on Pi at first but eventually realized that it was more flexible to perform it on a laptop. I tried so much to get downsampling to work to reduce the needed bandwidth. This is crucial for the slow Wi-Fi networks but particularly important when accessing your local network remotely via VPN through the internet. I did play a lot with resampling methods and reduced it to 11025 sample rate. It worked well and sounded fine for some time even though kept fading out after every two minutes. You can change your tunnel source to be the following (to downsample):

pactl load-module module-tunnel-source server=tau.partofthething source_name=icom_source rate=11025

pactl load-module module-tunnel-sink server=tau.partofthething sink_name=icom_sink rate=11025

This basically uses around 60KiB/s over the network and 200 KiB/s at default. You can change the sampling methods edit/etc/pulse/daemon.conf on Pi and adjust the resample-method=speed-float-1 setting.

In some resampling conditions, it is possible for PulseAudio to use the Pi's CPU excessively. The main problem however, is that there are a few delay seconds as the audio moves across the internet.

You can then unload each of the PA modules onto your PC using the following command (this is applicable if you are playing around with different settings).

```
pacmd unload-module 32
```

You can use the pacmd list-modules to make a list of all the loaded modules where 32 is the module's index to upload. You can do this a bunch as you tweak your script and rerun it.

Connect to the LAN securely with a VPN

A VPN enables you to connect to your local network over the internet remotely. And you can configure your Pi to make this connection possible.

You can conveniently set up a 'road warrior' OpenVPN on your WRT-based router. This in turn will allow you to connect to you home LAN anytime securely from anywhere. You will find this useful especially if you want to print things from far away, avoid surveillance while on public or other untrusted networks or talk to your internal devices. This step usually entails securing your WRT-compatible router, then using ROM that has OpenVPN server such as OpenWRT or DDWRT to flash it then creating some private or public keys and then proceeding to configure the clients and server. This is not entirely difficult, but can take you quite some time to get it working as a result of the numerous instructions that are a bit different -which are present online. The GUI-based config in current DDWRT builds makes it very simple. To know more about building some RSA Keys and flash your router, please visit this guide and perhaps also this guide as well.

Congratulations! I hope this project works for you as it was very incredible for me to figure out.

Download Your Free Bonus – 10 Best Ham Radio Websites

Conclusion

We have come to the end of the book. Thank you for reading and congratulations for reading until the end.

The numerous facets of amateur radio have managed to attract practitioners with many different interests worldwide. Many amateurs start with a simple fascination of radio communications but with time find themselves combining it with other deep-seated interests of their own to make the pursuit of their hobby fulfilling.

Regardless of whether you want to pursue the focal amateur areas such as radio propagation study, technical experimentation, radio contesting, public service communication or computer networking, having an understanding, and skills on amateur radio are sure to change your life, and broaden your perspective on so much that you had never imagined.

The book could not have possibly covered everything you need to know in the world of amateur radio; but you have a footing now. Do more research and try to more explore projects you can do to become a better practitioner, with Pi.

If you found the book valuable, can you recommend it to others? One way to do that is to post a review on Amazon.

Click here to leave a review for this book on Amazon!

Thank you and good luck!

Download Your Free Bonus – 10 Best Ham Radio Websites

Ham Radio Activities

The Complete Amateur Radio Contesting Manual

Tips & Techniques in a Ham Radio Contest

Introduction

I want to thank you and congratulate you for downloading the book, "*Ham Radio Activities: The Complete Amateur Radio Contesting Manual - Tips & Techniques in a Ham Radio Contest*".

This book is the ultimate amateur radio-contesting manual.

"Ham" that is the name given to those who operate ham radios. Ham radio contest, on the other hand, are a different ball game altogether.

In this guide, we shall be discussing how although the contest aspect of ham radio operation intimidates many, at the heart of the contest is the need for connection and fun.

This guide shall equip you with the requisite knowledge you need to participate in ham radio contests with skill and confidence. After learning the different types of contests, how they work and their rules, the software and hardware to use, you will start building up your QSO count and adding interesting DX contacts to your list of contacts.

Let's begin.

Thanks again for downloading this book. I hope you enjoy it!

© **Copyright 2018 by** _____ **- All rights reserved.**

This document is geared towards providing exact and reliable information in regards to the topic and issue covered. The publication is sold with the idea that the publisher is not required to render accounting, officially permitted, or otherwise, qualified services. If advice is necessary, legal or professional, a practiced individual in the profession should be ordered.

- From a Declaration of Principles which was accepted and approved equally by a Committee of the American Bar Association and a Committee of Publishers and Associations.

In no way is it legal to reproduce, duplicate, or transmit any part of this document in either electronic means or in printed format. Recording of this publication is strictly prohibited and any storage of this document is not allowed unless with written permission from the publisher. All rights reserved.

The information provided herein is stated to be truthful and consistent, in that any liability, in terms of inattention or otherwise, by any usage or abuse of any policies, processes, or directions contained within is the solitary and utter responsibility of the recipient reader.

Under no circumstances will any legal responsibility or blame be held against the publisher for any reparation, damages, or monetary loss due to the information herein, either directly or indirectly.

Respective authors own all copyrights not held by the publisher.

The information herein is offered for informational purposes solely, and is universal as so. The presentation of the information is without contract or any type of guarantee assurance.

The trademarks that are used are without any consent, and the publication of the trademark is without permission or backing by the trademark owner. All trademarks and brands within this book are for clarifying purposes only and are the owned by the owners themselves, not affiliated with this document.

Table of Contents

Introduction

Ham Radios Basics: Understanding Amateur Radio

   About Propagation

   About DX-Ing, Contests, and Awards

Contesting 101: A Cultural History of Amateur Radio Contesting

   About Contests

   Brief History of Amateur Radio Contesting

Getting Started: Getting Your Ham Radio License

   About FCC Licensing

   Licensing: About Frequency Privileges

   License Classes and their Various Transmission Privileges

   About The License Examination

   How to Prepare for the License Exam

Amateur Radio Competition Equipment

Making Your First QSO: A Simple, Ham Radio Contest Guide to Making Contacts

The Main Amateur Radio Contests and Their Rules

   ARRL DX Contest

   CQ World Wide DX Contest

   ARRL "Field Day"

Contesting Tips and Techniques for Better Amateur Radio Contesting

Conclusion

To get started, we shall go all the way back as a way to help you understand ham radios and their history.

Ham Radios Basics: Understanding Amateur Radio

Also called amateur radio, Ham radio is the use of select radio frequencies for communication. The communication can be private, emergency, non-commercial, or even for experimentation purposes.

The term "amateur" (as in Amateur Radio) refers to persons interested in radio technology for personal reasons (without any monetary interests) and to differentiate ham radio broadcasting from commercial broadcasting, professional two-way radio (such as those used by taxis, aviation, and marine), and public safety communication such as those used by the police and fire marshals. On the one hand, radio sport (also called contesting), is the competitive aspect of amateur radio where amateur radio operators (hams) compete against each other. An amateur radio operator is a person who uses radio equipment within an amateur radio station that has designated radio frequencies that have been assigned to an amateur radio service to engage other hams (amateur radio operators) in two-way personal communications.

To transmit on a specific radio frequency, amateur radio operators ought to pass an examination administered by a governmental authority, an examination that tests their grasp of applicable regulations, radio theory, electronics, and radio operation. Upon passing the exam, the hams get an amateur radio license.

One component of the license granted after passing the regulatory exam is a call sign that hams use for identifying themselves whenever they are communicating with other hams. According to the <u>International Amateur Radio Union, they are over 2.6 million amateur radio operators spread around the world.</u>

In a ham radio contest, hams, in teams or as individuals, use an amateur radio station (and its assigned frequencies) to contact, and exchange information with as many other amateur radio stations (other hams) within a specified time.

Each ham radio contest has its own rules that define the radio bands, the mode of communication used, as well as the kind of information exchanged during the contact. The contacts contacted throughout the said session make up a score that determines the ranking of each of the participating station.

As we have hinted at many times, hams use specific radio frequencies for communication. Because of the variety of frequencies, hams can use many frequency bands on the radio spectrum. In the U.S., the Federal Communications Commission (FCC) is responsible for allocating frequencies for amateur radio use.

For specificity purposes, hams can operate above the AM broadcast band and gigahertz range with many hams operating in the frequency range of AM radio band (1.6MHz) to slightly above the citizen band of 27MHz. To listen in to an amateur radio communication, non-hams can use radio scanners and receivers.

In the day, the best frequencies for long-distance communications are 15-27MHz. At night, the best frequency ranges for communication are 1.6-15MHz. From a historical perspective, bands within this range are what we call short-wave band (short-wave radio) and as you can guess, they are different from the frequencies used by most modern TV and radio stations.

Short-wave frequencies operate from a line-of-sight. Because of this, and because short waves bounce off the ionosphere from the transmitter to the antenna of the receiver, they have a limitation of 40-50 miles (the higher the frequency, the shorter the wavelength).

Other than using voice, some ham radio operators choose to use Morse code. As you may know, Morse code signals are more reliable and can get through when voice transmissions fail. If you choose to integrate the Morse code element into your ham radio learning experience, you will have to <u>learn Morse code</u>.

As we indicated earlier, Ham radio broadcast are different from normal radio broadcast. One of the key differences is that although ham radios can indeed broadcast in all directions (as a normal radio stations do when a DJ broadcasts a transmission to many tuned in listeners), ham radio communications are often two-way communications with other individual hams or in a roundtable setting of hams in a group.

Because of the short-range nature of the short wave, roundtable ham communications may be in the same town, state, country, continent, or even consist of a mixture of hams drawn from different countries depending on the time of day and the frequency in use.

At predetermined frequencies and times, hams also engage in networks called nets where they exchange third-party information and messages. For instance, when there are emergencies, hams exchange specific information such as health and welfare information.

When it comes to the equipment used by hams, hams use a variety of equipment some of which include radios and antennas with some hams choosing to use radioteletype (RTTY) that eliminate the use of teletype with computer screens.

In addition to using radios, hams also use telegraph equipment, cameras, laser, computers, and in the case of hams that offer professional services—such as those who offer emergency communication—their own satellites.

To the casual onlooker, the radios used by hams may seem very basic. While they are, they also use very sophisticated technologies (this should not dissuade you from engaging in the ham contests or being a ham enthusiast). In fact, many enthusiasts have varied background with some being experts in the field of technology while others know next to nothing. Think of operating a ham radio in the same way you think of computers: many can use it but very few know about how it works.

Some hams—especially those with a technology background—choose to create their own ham radio stations using equipment they design themselves. However, many hams choose to create ham stations using factory-built equipment that is readily available online and at stores countrywide. "Home brewing" is the name given to the process setting up a ham station and is one of the most enjoyable aspects of the hobby.

About Propagation

Propagation is one of the most important concepts in ham radios. The term refers to the process of the travel of radio waves through the air as they bounce from safe to surface as they make their way to a radio antenna.

Hams are constantly monitoring the atmosphere for atmospheric conditions such as storms, solar flares and other conditions that may affect the propagation or transmission of radio signals from receiver to antenna simply because the weather can affect the effectiveness of transmissions. This makes having the right equipment (especially an antenna because it's responsible for receiving radio signals) a requisite. A radio antenna can be complex or simple; it can be a massive tower or it can be something as simple as a wire attached to the circuitry of a radio.

While voice, Morse, and in the modern age, digital operations—most ham stations in existence today combine computers and radio equipment—and ham stations are the most commonly used types of ham radios and communication, from an operational perspective, most hams start out using VHF FM, battery-operated handheld transceivers that receive on one frequency and transmit on another.

To use these FM repeaters, ham enthusiasts have to join local radio clubs that set up and support them by borrowing antenna space from TV station towers (with permission of course) can re-broadcast received signals further thus extending the range.

For this purpose, the FM repeaters receive a signal at a time and immediately rebroadcast it to another frequency that is more powerful than what is available to the hand-held radio. This has the effect of extending the signal range of the hand-held radio. Many developed countries have thousands of FM repeaters and whenever you travel—or any ham radio enthusiast travels—you can find a repeater to use for communication.

Most of the available repeaters use common transmit and receive frequency pairs informally assigned by groups of hams so that any of the frequencies in use does not encroach on the frequency of another repeater and thus cause unwanted interference.

Other than hand-held transceivers and FM repeaters, ham radio enthusiasts also use amateur radio satellites. In this case, ham radio enthusiasts use a satellite overhead to communicate through their hand-held radios. This is very effective because as you may know, natural weather occurrences such as hurricanes or tornadoes tend to disrupt cellphone and telephone communication. In such instances, ham radios come in handy for emergencies. One British satellite repeater has an uplink (receiver) at 145.975 MHZ and a simultaneous downlink (rebroadcast) at 435.070 MHZ.

"Chewing the rag"

As we discussed earlier, from a contest perspective, the purpose of a ham radio contest is to contact as many people as possible. The communications most common in these conversations has a general reference term, "chewing the rag." When enthusiasts "chew the rag," the contacts they speak to become "ragchews," a term used to refer to a contact or the actual communication between hams. A ragchew—a contact or an actual conversation over the airwaves—can be between you and someone who lives down the street or someone who lives across the continent and is using advanced technology.

Earlier on, we also mentioned, in passing, nets. A net, short of network, is a predefined meeting of hams on a specific frequency dedicated to specific purposes. For instance, a net is a network that relays subject or topic specific message between operators. As an example, we have emergency nets that meet with the sole purpose of practicing preparedness for actual emergencies. We also have technical service nets that work as forums for ham operation advice and help hams work through the technical details of being ham operators.

About DX-Ing, Contests, and Awards

Meaning distance, DX is a very common term used by many ham radio enthusiasts. The term DX-ing means the practice of attempting contact with the person farthest away from you. For instance, if your antenna has a frequency of 50 miles, DX-ing would be attempting to establish contact with another ham at a 50-mile radius.

When it comes to contest and their awards, the ham world is exciting to the brim with many contests in existence. Most of these contests revolve around specific competition (such as DX-ing) or contacting as many people as possible within a given time. A later section of this guide shall cover contests and their rules.

A precursor to licensing

In this section, we have gotten basic information of ham radios, the culture, and a bit of the history. We shall have a detailed study of the history of ham radio contesting. For now though, before we can move on to the next section (where we'll discuss the cultural history of ham radio contesting), we need to talk a bit about contesting and the license requirements.

To become a ham radio operator, i.e. to be eligible to transmit on an amateur radio frequency, you need a license. This license is easy to enough (well, easy enough).

The test, administered in the U.S. by local volunteers, covers amateur radio rules and regulations as well as electronic theory. Because amateur radios have a vibrant community, you will find tons of study material and guides. The great thing about this license is that it does not have an age restriction (anyone can sit for the test: even children). Other countries and jurisdictions will have their own licensing bodies despite the fact that many countries share the same ham frequencies as those used in the United States.

The license has classes with each license class allowing operations within specific bands. Higher license classes allow the use of more frequency bands. In the U.S., the FCC has recently relaxed the Morse code requirements to make it easier for ham enthusiasts to get an amateur radio operator's license. While we shall have a section dedicated to licensing, the current FCC licensing plan will see you get an amateur radio license if you ace a 35-questions written examination.

Organized in 1914 by H.P. Maxim to help relay radio messages, the American Radio Relay League (ARRL) is without a doubt responsible for helping many enthusiasts get into amateur radio by publishing many study materials and publications. In the U.S., local volunteers who are members of amateur radio clubs are responsible for administering the amateur radio test.

Before we discuss ham radio equipment, let us discuss ham radio contests:

Contesting 101: A Cultural History of Amateur Radio Contesting

As implied earlier, radio sport (also called contesting) is the competitive side of amateur radio. The general aim of the contest is to contact and communicate with as many amateur radio stations as possible within a given time.

That said, contesting, more so the rules and nature of an amateur radio contest, changes from competition to competition with the most defining elements being the amateur bands used, the mode of communication, and the information exchanged during a ragchew. As also indicated earlier, the contacts made contribute to a score that the sponsors publish in a magazine or online publication.

Historically, contesting started developing in the 1920s and 30s from other amateur radio activities. As communication between amateur radio enthusiasts grew and expanded, competitions formed to motivate ham enthusiasts to contact as many amateur radio stations as possible in and outside their countries of residence.

The contest also formed as a way to provide hams an opportunity to practice and highlight their message handling abilities as used for emergency or even routine communications over extended distances. From these contests grew a wide number of contest and today, many amateur radio enthusiasts pursue it as a sporting activity.

Radio enthusiast magazines, radio societies, and radio clubs are the primary benefactors of amateur radio contests. Because sponsors are the organizers of the competitions, they are responsible for publishing the rules of the event. They are also responsible for collecting any operational logs from different stations that are participating in the event, cross checking the correctness of the data in order to generate a score for each of the stations, and publishing the result in a readily accessible platform such as a magazine, website, or society journal.

Most of the competitions—with the exceptions of specific contest for shortwave listeners—are between stations that have amateur radio licenses, and because of this, since most of the radio frequencies used in these competitions prohibit the use of radio frequencies for economic interests, these competitions are informal and there are no professional amateur radio contest or contesters. As such, when you participate in amateur radio competitions, do not expect cash rewards; instead, you will receive trophies, certificates, and perhaps plaques.

The most basic contest is where during a contest, each contest tries to establish two-way communication with other licensed hams on specific frequencies and exchange defined information specific to the nature of the contest.

In most of these contests, the information exchanged varies (its determined by the organizing body). For instance, the ragchew exchange between hams could be signal reports, the location of the station, the R-S-T system, the Maidenhead grid locator, the geographical location of the station, age of the operator, or a serial number.

For each contact made, the amateur radio operator must properly receive the call sign, a unique designation for a transmitter station assigned by the FCC (or any other government agency) or informally adopted by individuals or organizations. He or she must also receive and record in a log specific information defined in the rules of exchange (the information required to be exchanged), and a record of the time of the contact as well as the frequency used to make contact and exchange the information.

The organizing party then takes the log and uses the contacts to tabulate a score for each ham based on the score formula defined by that contest. The most common formula is one that assigns a number of each contact and a multiplier depending on the ragchew or information exchanged.

In contests held in North America on the VHF amateur radio bands, the most commonly used formula is one that assigns a new multiplier for individual (new) Maidenhead grid locator and thus, the competition winner is the one that makes most contacts with other stations in most locations.

Based on the rules of a particular contest, individual multipliers may count only once during the contest or once on each radio irrespective of the radio band that fist earned the multiplier. Because of this, the contest can affix a specific amount of points for each contact or depending on other factors such as the weather, geography and if the communication crossed boundaries such as political or continental.

Other contests award points depending on the points between two stations (the Stew Top Band Distance Challenge is a great example of such a contest). In Europe, most amateur radio contests held on the microwave and VHF award hams 1 point for each kilometer of distance, and therefore, the further the contact station, the higher the points.

After receiving the logs, the contest organizers check them for accuracy. At this point, they are free to deduct points, multiplier, and even credits if they note errors in the contact logs for individual contacts (QSO). As you can guess, the result of the score will largely depend on the scoring formula used. Some scores can be small numbers while others can be large numbers.

Most of ham radio contests in America and Europe have different entry categories. Each category has an individual winner with some contests segmenting winners by geography such as countries, Canadian provinces, continents, and U.S. States. Of these categories, the most common is the single operator category and its many variants.

In the single operator category, one ham operates an amateur radio station throughout the contest. The single operator category further divides into subdivisions depending on the highest power output. In one such division, the QRP category, single operator amateur radio stations must operate the station with no more than 5 watts of output power. The high power category of the single operator category allows hams to run stations that transmit with as much power output as allowed in their licenses.

If you want to get into ham radio as a team, you will have to get into the multi-operator category. This category allows hams to team up to operate a single amateur radio station. Some of the contests in this category ask hams to use one or several radio transmitters used simultaneously.

About Contests

From a contest perspective, different benefactors sponsor a variety of competitions each year with many of them (the sponsors) creating events whose purposes is to promote interest in ham radio as a hobby and requisite skill.

Weekends are the most common contest days. Some contests, however, also use local weeknight evenings. Some competitions are short while others are as long as 48 hours long (for a single session).

As hinted at earlier, each contest will define the stations eligible for participation, the frequencies of operation, the communication modes hams can employ, the frequencies of the amateur radio they should contact, and the time within which to make contact not to mention the information exchange with each contact station.

From this, it's clear to see that the rules of engagement depend on, and change from competition to competition. Some competitions will (and do indeed) restrict the contacts to specific standards such as continent and country (geographical). For instance, the European HF Championship has a sole aim: to foster competition between amateur radio stations in Europe.

Some contests allow amateur radio stations worldwide to participate and contact each other for points. One such contest is the CQ World Wide DX Contest that allows stations to contact other stations located anywhere on the planet. The competition attracts thousands of competition amateur radio stations each year.

Likewise, the amateur radio scene is full of regional contests that allow participation from stations spread across the world with the only restriction being the stations contacted by individual ham radio stations. An example of such a competition is the Japan International DX Competition. In the competition, Japan based amateur radio stations can only contact ham stations outside Japan and vice versa.

Most of the available contests use multiple (or one) amateur radio bands to allow stations in the competition to make two-way contacts. On various occasions, we have mentioned HF-based competitions. These competitions use either (as single or multiple bands) of the following bands; 160 meter, 80 meter, 40 meter, 20 meter, 15 meter, and 10 meter. VHF based contest use bands over 50 MHz.

In some contests, amateur radio stations can transmit on all HF and VHF bands with points awarded for multipliers and contacts on individual bands. Other contests may allow contacts on all bands but restrict the type of contact—perhaps to one contact with individual station irrespective of band, or place a limit on the multiplier to per contest instead of per band.

Amateur radio contests are available for amateur radio enthusiasts from all lifestyles. Some of these contests restrict themselves to CW emissions (meaning they us Morse code as their default mode of communication) while others restrict their communication to spoken communication (meaning they use telephony). Other contests use digital emission modes such as PSK31 or RTTY.

The most common thing in popular contests across the board is that most of them hold the contest on two separate weekends whether they dedicate one weekend to CW and the other to telephony. For instance, the CQ World Wide WPX Contest holds the phone-only contest on a weekend in March and the CW-only contest on a weekend in May.

Contest that restrict contact to single radio frequency bands often let competing amateur radio station use different [emissions modes](). Most VHF contests normally allow most (or any) emission mode even some digital modes designed to work on specific bands. Because content rules vary, some hams choose to specialize and participate in contests that restrict the use of certain modes.

Because of the nature of contest (the fact that each contest has specific rules) some contests can last up to 48 hours. The most common of such contests are those on the HF bands and contests open to worldwide participation. In most instances, these large (and worldwide) contests start at 0000 UTC on a Saturday morning to 2359 UTC Sunday. As you can imagine, smaller (especially regional ones) contest are shorter in duration with contests that last 4-24 hours being the most common.

Because of the duration of larger contests, some of them employ a concept called "off time" where a station can operate for a portion of the time available. An example of this is the ARRL November Sweepstake. Although the contest is 30 hours long, individual amateur radio station cannot be on air for more than 24 hours. The effect of the "off time" is that it forces competing stations to choose when to be online making contacts and logging them as well as when to be offline (or off air). This element adds strategy to the competition.

In the early 1930s, amateur radio contests could happen on multiple weekends. Although only a small number of contest have held on to this tradition (called cumulative contests), they limit themselves to Microwave frequency bands. To replace these types of contest, nowadays, the most popular types of contests are short "sprint" contest that last a few hours. Some contests such as the North American Sprint Contest increase the excitement and difficulty of the contest by requiring operators to change frequencies after making individual contacts.

As you get started in amateur radio contests, you will be looking for contests that allow newly licensed hams to compete. One such competition is the Maine 2 Meter FM Simplex Challenge. This challenge allows newly licensed hams to participate in contests; it does so by offering entry categories for those with handheld radios (or fully equipped contest stations) and restricting contacts to a singular VHF band.

Because we have a variety of contest, they attract many contestants and amateur radio stations. Because each contest defines its rules, the nature of the contest determines the strategies implemented by competing amateur radio stations to score the most points and multipliers.

Because each contest has specific sponsors who define rules of the contest, there lacks an international authority or governance organization for amateur radio as a sport. As such, there is not uniformity of contest rules. However, most of the contests appeal to all participants to adhere to amateur radio regulations of their individual states or countries.

Brief History of Amateur Radio Contesting

Amateur radio contesting traces back to the 1920 during the Trans-Atlantic Test where radio operators made the first attempted to use short wave radio frequencies to establish long distance communication across the Atlantic Ocean. In 1923, radio operators established the first two-way communication between Europe and North America. At that point, the tests become an annual event where many other stations started establishing two-way contacts over even greater distances.

In 1927, the American Radio relay League, a principle facilitator of the aforementioned tests, put forth a new formula for the annual event and at that point, started encouraging amateur radio stations to make as many two-way contacts with other stations in as many countries as they could.

1929 saw the first amateur radio contest dubbed the International Relay Party, a contest that was an immediate hit (and success). From 1927-1935, the ARRL sponsored the event and in 1936, changed the name of the event to ARRL International DX Contest, a name that event to date, represents one of the most vibrant amateur radio contests in the world.

Because of the growing interest generated by the popularity DX communication through participation in International Relay Parties, the ARRL proposed and then adopted an event format for non-international contacts.

In 1930, ARRL started the first ARRL All-Sections Sweepstakes Contest, a contest that required a robust exchange of information for all contacts made from two-way contacts, a formula adopted from the National Traffic System (its message header structure).

Because of the robustness of the information exchange, the competition grew in popularity with many operators using it as a way to gauge their operating skills and the robustness of their stations. The event became a primary attraction for those with amateur radio competition in their minds and in 1962, the ARRL sponsored event took on the name ARRL November Sweepstakes.

[Field day](#) operating events are some of the most important developments in early amateur radio contesting, with one of the earliest organized field day event held in 1930 in Great Britain, and event later mirrored by many small field day events held across Europe and North America. In July 1933, ARRL organized the first ARRL International Field Day, an event the league popularized through the OST, their growing membership journal.

ARRL promoted field day events as an opportunity for amateur radio enthusiasts to test their emergency and disaster preparedness where they would have to operate from portable locations. Since then, field day events continue to be popular mainly because even though they use the same operating and scoring structures used by other amateur radio contest, they add in an element of disaster or emergency preparedness.

Most modern day amateur radio contests draw heavily on the custom of DX communications, communication readiness, and traffic handling. Since the 1920s, as interest in ham radio activities has grown, so has the amateur radio contest.

In the 1930, radio societies in countries such as Spain, Canada, Australia, and Poland took sponsorship or amateur radio contests. In specific, the 1934, the ARRL sponsored a contest event restricted to the 10-meter amateur radio band. As 1937 dawned, countries such as Zealand, Brazil, Hungary, France,

Ireland, Germany, and Great Britain say an influx of sponsored contests.

The first ever VHF contest held was in 1948, a contest dubbed the ARRL VHF sweepstake. On the other hand, the RTTY society of Southern California was the first to organize the first RTTY contest in 1957. The National Contest Journal, a publication that started circulating in the United States in 1973, was the first publication specifically dedicated to the sport of amateur radio.

In terms of international contests, the IARU HF World Championship, an event sponsored by the Amateur radio Union and previously called the IARU Radiosport Championship (a name changed in 1986), started in 1977.

In 1986, as amateur radio become popular as a sport, CQ amateur radio Magazine started the Contest Half of Fame. As time went by and the sport's popularity grew, its popularity worldwide grew and tens of thousands of hams started connecting their ham radios, conventions, journals, and websites.

Because the sport does not have a worldwide organizing authority or body, the sport lacks a world ranking system and as such—and because contesters cannot compare themselves to other hams—the challenges faced by competitors depend on locality, proximity to amateur radio communities, and most importantly, the radio propagation rules of the location.

July 1990 was an exciting month because in this month, the world witnessed the first ever "face to face" championship known as World Radiosport Team Championship, an event held in Seattle Washington, an event whose purpose was to overcome some of the challenges presented by previous amateur radio competitions.

The contest saw the participation of top hams from around the globe and required them to participate in the competition from a single location. In the event, 22 teams of 2 persons represented fifteen countries with some from the Soviet Union and the Eastern bloc.

In 1996, San Francisco California played host to another WRTC event; in 2000, Bled, Slovenia played host; in 2002, Helsinki, Finland took the mantle; and in 2006, Florianópolis, Brazil played host to the WRTC. The version of the event that most hams consider the "world championship" took place in 2010 in Moscow Russia.

Learn more about current WRTC events from the resource link below:

http://www.wrtc2018.de/index.php/en/

For a more detailed history of how the technology has developed from the beginning to its present states, read the valuable and insightful resource below:

http://w2pa.net/HRH/

Now that we have a fairer understanding of ham radio contest, the next thing we need to look at is how to get started:

Getting Started: Getting Your Ham Radio License

The last two sections clearly outlined the need for a ham radio license. As the previous sections implied, although the licensing test is simple, at first glance, it may seem confusing and chaotic.

This section of the guide shall walk you through the process of getting your ham radio license because without it, you cannot participate in amateur radio contests. Even when your reasons for involving yourself in ham radio activities may not be contest related, you still need a license if you intend to use your ham radio to send two-way messages.

About FCC Licensing

As implied earlier in this guide, as a US resident, you can get your ham radio license from the Federal Communications Commission (FCC), the federal body governing the ham radio or Amateur Radio Service.

The FCC has three license offerings: (***1***) ***the technician license class***, (***2***) ***the general license class***, and (***3***) ***the extra license class***. The first class, the technician license class, is the introductory license. Before you can earn any of the other licenses, you must earn it.

The main difference among the license classes is the transmit frequency privileges. When the FCC issues a license in any of the classes, it gives the license holder the privilege of transmitting on specific range of frequencies allocated to amateur radio service. The further you climb up the license classes, the broader the frequencies on which you can transmit with the extra license class allowing a license holder full use of all frequencies dedicated to amateur radio services.

Licensing: About Frequency Privileges

As you can probably note from the above discussions, the different license classes offer different transmission frequencies. Each of the licenses and frequencies dictates the type of on air-operations you can conduct. It is, therefore, very important to understand the various license classes because that understanding will help get you off to a great start as a ham radio enthusiast.

Before we can delve into the various licenses classes and what each allows you to transmit, we need to backtrack a bit and cover basic radio concepts that will help you understand the differences in license classes and their in-built on air operation.

About Frequency Bands

A frequency band is a contiguous range of radio frequencies. Simply put, radio signals, which are what your ham radio sends out and receives, utilize magnetic and electric fields to hop from antenna to antenna. The frequency is the rate at which a signal travels back and forth.

Licensees of the technician class license use radio frequencies expressed in millions of back and forth cycles per second (or in some cases, hundreds of millions of cycles per second). The unit of measuring the cycle per second is hertz and that of millions of cycles/second is megahertz (MHz), something we have mentioned in passing many times in this guide.

To simplify this concept even further, consider a signal that wiggles from 144 MHz to 148 MHz on a frequency band. From a nontechnical perspective, your FM radio has a commercial frequency band of 88 MHz to 108MHz; you can use your tuner to access any of the radio stations transmitting within these frequencies.

Just as the FCC has allocated specific frequency bands to commercial FM radios, it has allocated such frequency bands to Amateur Radio Services; these frequencies are what we call ham bands; each frequency band within the ham band will have a different propagation or traveling characteristic.

About Operating Mode

The AM and FM bands on your car or home radio are two different operating modes: the amplitude modulation (AM) and the frequency modulation (FM). These two modes are different in that they use different encoding mechanisms to transmit information into radio signals.

Learn more about AM and FM operating mode from the following resource:

https://www.diffen.com/difference/AM_vs_FM

Ham radios use AM and FM modes as well as other modes such as Morse code and computer-generated digital packets among many other digital modes. In essence, a mode is the system used to transmit information to and from a radio wave.

Now that you understand this, let us look at license classes and the various things each license class allows you to do:

License Classes and their Various Transmission Privileges

Earlier, we introduced three license classes:

(1) The general license class

(2) The technician license class

(3) The extra license class

As we go through the license classes, use the US Amateur Radio Bands Chart as a reference:

Technician license

As implied earlier, this is the entry-level license. Once you get this license, you immediately gain access to amateur radio frequency bands of up to 30 million cycles/second and higher, radio frequencies normally regarded as VHF (Very High Frequency), UHF (Ultra High Frequencies) and higher microwave frequencies. With access to these bands, you can use them for voice modes such as FM and AM and even for digital modes such as Morse code.

Normally, VHF frequencies (and other high frequencies) travel further than line-of-sight and are thus what we call locally propagating signals. On these frequencies, if you have a powerful antenna placed on a high mast, you can transmit and receive signals over many miles with the distance depending on the terrain of the area. As we also implied earlier, many areas have repeaters that allow for the extension of the range of communication.

With a technician license class, you can participate in local nets or on air meetings that involve several hams and in cases where the hams you connect with are using repeaters, you can communicate with hams in different states (of course depending on the terrain and your equipment range). To increase the distance of communication, some hams use their VHF and UHF privileges and satellite repeaters orbiting earth.

A technician class license limits your privileges on high frequency bands (bands in HF, 3 to 30 MHz). As you know, there is a difference in propagation of the different frequencies. For instance, HF frequencies will propagate differently from VHF or UHF.

On their part, high frequencies can reflect on the ionosphere, a layer of earth's atmosphere, and thus travel further, even around the globe. The technician license allows you to transmit voice on a HF band of 10-meter band and Morse code on 4HF bands. Essentially, this means that with this license, you can contact other hams in different countries across the world.

General License

As stated earlier, to earn this license, you need to earn the technician one; this license simply expands the privileges of the technician license by allowing you access to additional operating modes and higher frequency bands.

When you earn this license, you can operate on all amateur bands allocated to amateur radio services by the FCC. You can use voice modes on all allowed HF bands (7 HF bands), which allows you to make voice contacts over greater distances—again, using the ionospheric skip propagation—and can also use Morse code and other digital modes in 8 HF bands that propagate around the world.

Extra License

This license expands the privileges of the general class. It allows the use of extra class exclusive band segments and essentially, gives you access higher frequencies whose propagation exceeds the local area. Because this class offers more communication possibilities, it requires more skills and technical knowhow.

For the remainder of this section, we shall restrict our discussion to the technician class license because although it's an entry level license, it offers a ton of frequencies and communication capabilities.

About The License Examination

To earn any of the three licenses, you have to pass an examination. Each of the classes has an examination that tests your grasp of amateur radio rules, operating procedures, regulations, and other technical topics.

The questions for each license come from a pool of exam questions with each question revised every 4 years. The questions for the latest technician class license come from a questions pool created in July 1, 2014 and that will remain valid until June 30, 2018. The questions are often simple and the public domain for the development of study guides and material.

The current entry-level class license has a pool of 426 multiple questions. However, the exam itself has 35 questions selected from the pool and where after reading the questions, you choose option A, B, C, or D as the correct answer to the questions. To pass the technician exam, you must score a pass rate of 74% (or get right 26 out of the 35 questions).

In modern day, these exams do not require a demonstrated ability to communicate in Morse code and thus, to get a license—whichever license class—all you have to do is pass the multiple-choice question exam.

The National Conference of Volunteer Examiner Coordinators (NCVEC) is the body responsible for formulating the questions pool and their volunteer examiners (VEs) are the ones responsible for administering the exam across the United States. These volunteer VEs are ham enthusiasts certified and sanctioned by the FCC.

Where To Find An Examination Session

If you live in a populated locality that has a vibrant ham radio community, you will find several exam sessions held each month at ham radio events of held by ham radio clubs. If you live in a densely populated area that lacks a vibrant ham radio community, you may have to travel a short distance to attend an examination.

Use the following resources to search for scheduled VE exams:

http://www.arrl.org/find-an-amateur-radio-license-exam-session

http://www.w5yi.org/exam_locations_ama.php

Most VE administered exams allow walk ins; however, some will require an advance registration.

What To Bring To The Exam Room

When going to sit for the exam, you will need to carry with you, a driver's license (or any other state issued photo ID such as your social security card—if you have one—student ID, birth certificate, utility bill, and the likes). You will also need to carry money ($15) for the fee payment, a calculator, and pencils.

How to Prepare for the License Exam

How you prepare for the exam will determine how great you manage. Here, you have various options: you can memorize enough questions to pass the exam, which is not a great strategy because even though you may ace the exam, you will not have a clear or firm understanding of the concepts and radio terminologies.

Learning and understanding the ham radio and the concepts behind it is the best study strategy because it allows you to understand what the exam questions are asking of you, which will allow you to figure out the right answers.

To study for the exam (and learn more about ham radios), you can use study guides or attend a class offered by ham radio clubs. You can find study guides on the resources below:

http://www.kb6nu.com/study-guides/

https://hamstudy.org/

http://www.aclog.com/aprs/study.php

Amateur Radio Competition Equipment

Now that you have your technician class license, to get started, the other thing you need to do (if you have not) is to set up your equipment and station. At the most basic level, you will need a ham radio that can transmit and receive signals using the various modes.

In this section, we shall discuss the various equipment you need to participate in ham radio contests. We shall start with the basics:

Transceivers

To get started immediately, this guide recommends that you get an FM transceiver. Because the technician class offers you access to VHF and UHF frequencies and repeaters on which is the most popular voice mode, FM, you can use an FM transceiver to send noise-free voice messages in a trouble free manner.

Most available handheld transceivers are FM only, so are most of the transceivers in cars—mobile operations—or the ones used to create a base station. Most of these transceivers restrict themselves to 1-3 VHF-UHF amateur bands.

Another option here is a multimode transceiver. These types of transceivers are a bit pricey but offer complex operations and capabilities. To transmit voice over HF bands, you will need a transceiver that has a <u>single sideband mode</u>. This mode is very special in that it optimizes use of power and is the most popular for long distance communications on HF bands as well as over-the-horizon voice transmission.

A multimode transceiver is ideal for when you upgrade your license to the general class license because the license expands the phone mode privileges on the HF bands. Further, the transceiver (a multimode transceiver) allows you to communicate in Morse code as well as attach a computer for transmissions on digital modes.

Now that you have your technician class license, get a radio. The most commonly used transceivers are the handheld HTs.

Commonly called HTs or handy-talkies by most hams, you can start out by buying a FM HT that offers 2-meter band on VHF and 70-centimeter band on UHF. These are the most commonly used handheld transceivers since most available repeaters use these frequency ranges. With that said, some parts of the

United States use the 1.25-meter band for repeater operations.

While you can start with the most basic HT (which transceiver you start out with shall depend on your level of knowledge and expertise), you have many radio choices with many radios offering various inclusions and features. For starters—especially if you are relatively new to ham radios—go for a HT radio that does not appear too complicated (they are easier to manipulate and are not as expensive). If you are unsure of which HT to buy to get started, join a club or seek the mentorship of an Elmer (an experienced ham radio operator).

Learn more about buying transceivers from the following resources:

http://rsgb

http://rsgb

In closing this transceiver section though, we have to mention that purchasing radios is perhaps the most costly aspect of setting up an amateur radio station primarily because the radio is very central to ham radio activities. This therefore means that choosing the right transceiver/radio is very important (which is why this guide suggests that if you are unsure of which radio to buy, to seek assistance from an Elmer).

Now that you have chosen a radio, you also need to pay some attention to filters. A filter allows you full use of a desired radio signal while reducing the signal strength of other signals in your locality.

Now that you're setting up your amateur radio station, you will need a good filter because an effective one makes ham radio operations and communications easier. Whether you need to buy a filter will depend on the type of transceiver you choose to use since radios offer cascading filters that follow one another while others provide extra filters.

In addition to a transceiver, you may need one or any of the following (depending on your chosen transceiver).

Power Supply

If you opt to start out on a handheld transceiver, one you can use on UHF (FM or VHF, you will need rechargeable batteries (read the device manual to know the type of power supply you need for your handheld transceiver).

If you decide that you'll set up the transceiver at a specific area of your home, you shall need to invest in a DC power supply whose voltage shall depend on the voltage needs of your transceiver (most handheld transceivers have a voltage requirement of 13.8 volts and you may need to buy an adapter.

If you have a base station—a permanent or mobile one—you will need a power supply of no less than 13.8 volts (check the device manual for voltage specifications). Some base stations will come equipped with a 230 volts power supply inbuilt. Most transceivers will have a manual telling you the maximum voltage for individual devices so that the power supply you get is adequate.

The types of power supplies in the market are switched-mode and linear. The linear type has a bulky design that uses two transformers to change the input voltage of 230 volts into 13.8 DC power for use by the base station. Linear power supplies are heavy and large.

The switched-mode ones are vastly different in that they directly convert the AC voltage into DC and then filter it. The High voltage DC is subsequently fed into a power oscillator, which usually switches it on or off at a frequency of 20 to 50 kHz with the result being a pulsating DC converted to 13.8 volts by a transformer. Switched mode power supplies are smaller, lighter, and cheaper than linear power supplies. However, even though these power supplies are smaller and cheaper, take note that in some instances, they may interfere with signals transmitted over your radio. To ensure zero signal interference, choose a switched-mode power supply that has a low radio frequency interference (RFI) feature or one that has a knob you can use to adjust interference when you note it.

Coax

A coax shall help you connect your antenna and transceiver. Since most radios have a 50 Ohm unbalanced output, you will need a 50-Ohm coax.

Before you buy a coax, you should give proper thought to the quality of the coax you intend to buy and its characteristic losses. In this regard, note that the higher the frequency, the greater the coax loss. For operating on lower HF bands, a 5mm RG58 coax will suffice. When you move to the higher high frequency bands of 24-28 MHz or 144-430 MHz, you will need a better coax.

The most commonly used coax is the RG213 because other than offering lower losses, it's also less flexible and thicker.

Antennas and Antenna Analyser/SWR meter

The antenna you choose to use for your base station can be directional or omnidirectional. Directional antennas beam concentrated signals in one direction while omnidirectional ones radiate the signal out equally. If you have a mobile transceiver, you'll note that it uses whip antennas you can interchange for different bands.

Most modern transceivers have inbuilt SWR meters that help with the setting up of an antenna. Additionally, many external antennas units have inbuilt SWR meters that make finding matches easier.

If you are assembling a base station in a car, you will need an SWR meter so you can correctly set up the antenna. The same case applies to a home base station; when choosing which one to buy, consider the bands you will be transmitting on.

Further to this, if you will be experimenting with different types of antennas, you will need an analyser, which although not cheap, will be very essential and offer more information—such as faults in cables, measure of the cable electrical length, and a graphical display of the SWR curve—than an SWR ever could.

The first antenna you set up should be a half-wave dipole antenna.

To learn more about setting up your first antenna, read the content on the invaluable resource below:

http://rsgb.org/main/get-started-in-amateur-radio/antennas/your-first-antenna-the-half-wave-dipole/

Log Book

Since you will be participating in amateur radio contest, and while it is not a necessity, you will need a log book where you can log your contacts. The most inexpensive way to keep a log is to have a paper log. However, for contest purposes (which is the purpose of this guide), it's important to have a computer log. Fortunately, there're plenty of software (for both Mac and PCs) with some being paid and some free.

While a paper log is easy to keep, an electronic one is ideal for competitions because it automatically logs all you contacts and the ragchew exchange between you and the other station. To add to this, most of the available logging software also print labels for your QSL cards, track your progress towards any goals (if you're in a contest), and also upload the log or information to the ARRL's logbook.

To learn more about logging software, see the content on the resources below:

https://en.wikipedia.org/wiki/List_of_amateur_radio_software

http://www.w1wc.com/software/

https://www.dxzone.com/5-free-ham-radio-logbook-programs/

To learn more about the equipment you need for ham radio competition, as well as the various logging software available, read page 5-15 of this free contesting manual:

http://k4ro.net/w4phs/W4PHS_Guide_to_Ham_Radio_Contests.pdf

Making Your First QSO: A Simple, Ham Radio Contest Guide to Making Contacts

Now that you've set up your base station and you're ready to start contacting other station, you're ready to make your first contact (your first QSO). Before making your first on-air radio contact, this book recommends that you listen in to a few conversations. If you're in the vicinity of a repeater, monitor it and then tune it to the ragchew exchange between the other hams to note the type of conversation going on, the language used, and such. Most ragchew exchanges will use common language with a few ham radio specific terms thrown in there.

The easiest way to learn the lingo is by looking over the resource below that has a list of common ham radio terms:

http://www.hamradioschool.com/wp-content/uploads/2014/04/common_ham_radio_terms.pdf

After listening in for a while and when you feel ready to make your first contact, use the knowledge you used from your exam study guide to make the first on-air contact by pushing-to-talk and using your new call sign—

assigned to you after passing your technician license test.

While your first QSO can be daunting—not to mention the anxiety that comes with contacting experienced hams when your just a newt—you can arrange to test the waters by arranging your first QSO with a friend, perhaps one from the club, or an Elmer if you have one. This will make the prospect less stressful and instead fill it with fun.

In addition, this guide recommends that you get started by making your first QSO on a 2m FM instead of a HF SSB because the latter can be noisier and prone to interference.

Before you get started—this applies whether you're contacting other hams for fun or are in a contest—you need to make sure your radio is on the right mode, you have the right amount of power, and that the microphone gain is correct. Make sure, also, that you're using the correct antenna that matches your needs and radio. Here, you can use an ATU or feed the line directly into your radio. For the latter, ensure that the antenna has a low SWR.

If you intend to make a phone or voice QSO, you will have to (1) call CQ or (2) answer someone who is actually calling CQ. What does

CQ mean? Well, a CQ is a general call targeted at no one in particular and is the traditional ham radio way of reaching out to new ham radio contacts. Obviously, before you make or receive a CQ call, you need to find a frequency not in use by another station, which is usually not easy especially if you live in a ham radio vibrant locality where there's crowding on the HF bands.

About Finding An Open Frequency

Finding an open frequency is a process. The first thing you need to do is tune your antenna tuner to as close as 1:1 as you can and then check to see if someone is using the frequency. Not hearing something is not an indicator of a frequency not in use. Someone could be using a frequency, say nothing, but still hear you.

To check if a frequency is in use, send "QRL" (a term used to ask if the frequency is in use or if the ham on the other side is busy) and if you're on voice, simply state, *"This is (insert your call sign here). Is this frequency busy?"* Depending on the reply you get, either move on or use the frequency if you don't hear a response.

The key idea here is to listen before talking or transmitting.

To call CQ, use the 3 X 3 method. In the 3 X 3 method, you call CQ three times in the format below:

"CQ CQ CQ this is Dave Six Alpha Bravo Charlie, Dave Six Alpha Bravo Charlie, Dave Six Alpha Bravo Charlie standing by."

When you use this formula, a station may come back to you and say:

"N1ABC (or whatever) N1ABC, this is Dave Six Alpha Bravo Charlie. Good evening/day, your report is 59 (or whatever it is), my name is Mike – Delta Alpha Victor Echo – and my QTH is London – Lima Oscar November Delta Oscar November."

NOTE: It's important to point out here that the informational exchange will vary from contest to contest. Some contacts will come back to you with your report, name, and QTH while others will not. For competition purposes, its important to note the kind of information needed in the exchange so that if a station does not offer that information, you can ask questions to get it.

Other than taking note of the above as it relates to competition, what you talk about with your new contact will vary. For instance, you can exchange information about your stations, on whatever else you want.

The point of note here is that you should conduct yourself with decorum, as if anyone in the world is tuning into your conversation, which is not a too farfetched notion because in the real sense, anyone could be listening in. As such, avoid conversations around hot topic that draw out the worst in people—politics and religion are prime examples of topics to avoid or terminate when they start turning into arguments.

In some instances, especially if you've established a QSO contact with a station operated by a non-English speaking person, the other ham will wish you a "73" and move on. 73 is a Q code for best wishes and in this case, it simply means the person operating the station is non-English speaking and is wishing you well because he or she does not want to get tongue tied. 73 is also an ideal way to end a conversation.

Check the resource below for a full list of QR codes:

http://www.amateur-radio-wiki.net/index.php?title=Codes_and_Alphabets

Please note that for contest, you need to understand the contest rules so you can know which information to exchange when you make your QSO.

After making your first QSO and accustoming to operating your ham radio, using repeaters and radio bands, and contacting other hams directly without using repeaters (called talking to other ham simplex), you can then consider upgrading to something that has a higher power output than the handheld. The more you immerse yourself in the ham universe, the faster and better your skills shall grow, and the more effective you shall be when competing. You will also have a ton of fun.

Now that you know as much as the next ham, the other thing we shall talk about are the various types of contests, their rules, and past winners.

The Main Amateur Radio Contests and Their Rules

Now that you're immersing yourself in the ham universe—not to mention getting better at making contacts and operating your station (practice makes perfect)—you will be looking to get into the exciting world of amateur radio contesting.

The great thing about amateur radio is that it has a vibrant community and because of this, you will never lack a contest to participate in; in fact, at any given moment, you may find a contest underway in almost any part of the world.

In this section of the guide, we shall discuss the main amateur radio contests held during the year, when they happen, their rules, and past winners.

ARRL DX Contest

The purpose/mission of this contest it to encourage stations to enhance their knowledge of DX propagation on HF and MF bands and improve their operating skills. The contest also seeks to improve hams and station capabilities because the completion seeks to have DX stations only contact W/VE stations. W/VE stations are stations operating in the United

States and the District of Columbia (minus Hawaii and Alaska), and most Canadian territories and provinces except those on Sable and St. Paul Island.

The contest defines DX stations as any non-W/VE station including those in the US and territories such as the Pacific and Caribbean. It defines DXCC entities as those defined by the ARRL DXCC list. The contest demands an electronic log submitted by email or a memory device. It defines an automated multi-channel decoder—such as CW skimmer—as a device that reveals information about the frequency and identity of the contest station without the direct control and participation of operating ham.

The contest happens on:

CW: the 3rd full weekend in February (for instance, February 17-18, 2018)

Phone: The 1st full weekend in March (for example, March 3-4, 2018)

The entry categories for the contest are single operator, single operator unlimited, single operator single band, and multioperator.

The required informational exchange between contacts and stations has to be:

W/VE stations send signal reports and province or state while DX stations send signal reports as well as a number showing transmitter output power.

When it comes to scoring, points for contacts (QSO) are three for W/VE stations per DX QSO and three for W/VE QSO. For the multipliers, for the W/VE stations, the points depend on the sum of DXCC entities per band (except for those located in U.S. and Canada) while for DX stations, the contest scoring rules states this:

"Sum of US states (except KH6/KL7), District of Columbia (DC), and Canadian provinces/territories: NB (VE1, 9), NS (VE1), QC (VE2), ON (VE3), MB (VE4), SK (VE5), AB (VE6), BC (VE7), NT (VE8), NF (VO1 – see note, LB (VO2 – see note), NU (VY0), YT (VY1), PE (VY2) worked per band (maximum of 63 per band). Note – although VO1 and VO2 have been officially merged into a single province, they are counted separately in this contest for reasons of tradition."

The final score is a sum total of the QSO points multiplied by a total of the multipliers.

To learn more about this contest, the general rules of engagement, as well as previous and upcoming events, check out the resources below:

Arrl

Rules for arrl contests

Rules for arrl contests below 30-MHz

Rules for arrl contests above 50-mhz

You can see records of past winners from the resource below:

http://www.arrl.org/contest-records

CQ World Wide DX Contest

Held on the last full weekend of October for the SSB and the last full weekend of November for the CW, the aim of this contest is for amateur ham enthusiasts to contact as many stations as they can in all CQ zones and countries (or as many as they can).

The contest allows the use of 6 bands: 1.8, 3.5, 7, 14, 21 and 28 MHz and encourages contestants to observe the established bands. For the exchange, the SSB contest asks contestants to exchange RS report and the CQ zone number of the station contacted; for the CW contest, contestants must exchange the RST report and the CQ zone.

When it comes to scoring, the final score is the total contact (QSO) points multiplied by sum of zone and location/country multipliers. To earn QSO points, contesters can only contact a station once on each band and normally depend on the location of the station contacted.

For contacting a station in a different continent, hams earn 3 points. For contacting a station within the same continental bounds, but in a different country, a station earns 1 point with the exception being the award of 2 points for contacting stations in different countries within the Northern American boundaries. Contacting stations within the same country does not earn you QSO points but count as zone and country multiplier credit.

The contest has two types of multipliers. The first one is an application of a multiplier of 1 for each contact made on each band for different CQ zones. The second is a country multiplier of 1 for different stations contacted from different countries on each band.

The contest allows the following entry categories; single operators, single operator assisted, QRP assisted, classic operator, rookie, and multi-operators.

You can learn more about this contest, rules and regulations, future contest dates, as well as past winners from the resources below:

https://www.cqww.com/rules.htm

https://www.cqwpx.com/

https://www.cqwpx.com/score_db.htm

ARRL "Field Day"

Held on the last weekend in June, the objective of this contest is for amateur radio stations to contact as many amateur radio stations on all amateur radio bands excluding those on the 12, 17, 30 and z60-meter bands. The secondary aim is for hams to learn how to operate their stations in non-optimal conditions.

The competition is open to all participants in countries within in the IARU region 2 and all areas covered by the ARRL/RAC field organization. You can contact other stations outside these areas for credit.

You can learn more about this field day event from the following resource:

http://www.arrl.org/field-day

To know which contest is happening when—not to mention the rules for each contest—use the resource below:

http://www.contestcalendar.com//contestcal.html

The following resource also has a free guide that outlines various aspects of contesting and rules:

http://k4ro.net/w4phs/W4PHS_Guide_to_Ham_Radio_Contests.pdf

In closing this section, it's important to point out that competitions you can engage in are many; each will have a different set of rules. Read a summary of the rules for the content you intend to enter and then download a complete version of the rules so you can assess them.

In addition to following contest specific rules, take note and adhere to FCC rules as well as good operating practice and ham radio etiquette.

Contesting Tips and Techniques for Better Amateur Radio Contesting

Tips to help you improve your ham radio expertise are many. In this section, we shall discuss specific tips that applied, shall help you win more contests (and enjoy them more).

Look Over The Contest Details Beforehand

This is perhaps the most important tip in this book. You don't want to go into a contest blind, which is why you should look over the contest details, rules, times, and other such things before you go about entering into a contest. The most important thing to check is the time of the contest—given that the have different time zones, synchronize the time of the contest with your time zone—as well as the rules of the contest. You also need to understand the information you need to submit on the log because they change from contest to contest.

It also a good idea to look over past contest winners to understand the top scores for the previous year. This will give you an idea of the scores to aim for as you participate in the competition as well as the scores that count as credible.

Test Your Equipment

This is just as important as the tip above. Because competitions are fierce, you should test your equipment before entering into a competition to make sure everything is in proper working order. Particularly, check out the antenna system (and if need be, install a new one or improve upon your current one).

Check the antenna for corrosion—antennas left outside have a tendency to wear and because of it, lose their effectiveness—and especially check the joints and connections.

To earn more points in contests:

Always Go For Multipliers First

While QSO points are important, those that add to the multiplier count have more weight. Because of this, as you compete, specifically seek out, and contact multiplier stations (of course depending on the contest rules) before contacting other types of stations. Some loggers such as the N1MM will highlight multipliers in red from the spotting list and have a separate screen that shows multipliers available on a band.

Be Mindful Of Where You Tune

When checking through your spotting list of stations, take care not to go outside the frequencies defined by the contest rules and your licensed frequency range. For instance, if you're competing in the general class ticket, take care not to contact stations in the extra class region and if you have an extra class ticket, take care not to go outside the U.S. frequency bands.

As a general class operator, to avoid extra and advanced regions that are on the lower end of the bands, start at the lowest, legally acceptable frequency in this class band and then work your way up towards the higher frequencies.

Work As Many Stations In Similar Directions

If you're using a directional antenna, an effective strategy is to point the antenna in one direction that shows multiple stations, work down the spotting list (of course the stations you contact shall depend on the contest rules) and contact as many stations as possible.

Once done with that block of stations, swing the antenna in another direction and repeat the process. For instance, if you point your antenna towards China, work all the stations in that region, then swing it towards Europe, and repeat the process.

Work Through Searching And Pouncing

If you implement the tip above, you should have a healthy list of contacts to work through. When your list dries up, don't spend most of your time calling CQ. Instead, search, pounce, and then when you have a healthy list, run again.

Breaks Are Important

As we indicated earlier, some contests can last as long as 48 hours. While participating in such contests, it's important to take occasional refreshing breaks. Being too tired will not help you win a contest; instead, it will take the fun out of contesting.

Conclusion

We have come to the end of the book. Thank you for reading and congratulations for reading until the end.

From everything we have discussed in this guide, you can see that ham radios are fun (and a very useful skill to have) and engaging in contest is but a fun way to enhance your amateur radio knowledge and expertise.

Once you work through the formative parts of your entry into the wonderful world of amateur radio, work your way into contesting as a way to challenge yourself and enhance your operational and technical knowledge as well as your ability to make contacts in different situations and scenarios.

If you found the book valuable, can you recommend it to others? One way to do that is to post a review on Amazon.

Click here to leave a review for this book on Amazon!

Thank you and good luck!

Printed in Great Britain
by Amazon